architecture

KAZUYO SEJIMA + RYUE NISHIZAWA SANAA

yuko hasegawa

Electaarchitecture

translation
Richard Sadleir
Setsuko Miura

editorial coordination
Giovanna Crespi

graphic design and layout
Tassinari/Vetta
Roberta Leone

editing
Gail Swerling

cover design
Tassinari/Vetta

Distributed by Phaidon Press
ISBN 190431340X
ISBN 9781904313403

www.phaidon.com

www.electaweb.it

Contents

An Architecture of Awareness for the Twenty-First Century

Yuko Hasegawa

Introduction

Rem Koolhaas says that "weightless architecture" is nomadic and personal (not public), in the Deleuzian sense.

It is difficult to analyze the complexity, ambiguity, and looseness concealed in the simplicity of SANAA's architecture. One way is to utilize key words such as lightness, flexibility, and the brief. To understand how they explore unknown fields liberated from conventional architectural concepts, it would be far more interesting to examine how their architectural works are used over a period of time.

Kazuyo Sejima worked in the Toyo Ito office for six years. She had a project called "Pao II – Pao: A Dwelling for Tokyo Nomad Women." When she left Ito's office and constructed her first work, Platform, Sejima spoke out about the project. She said that the Pao did not achieve its goal, to achieve "Weightless Transportation." When she entered the Pao, she felt an oppressive heaviness. She said she intended to create a weightlessness and openness that were simply not there.[1] Her works are not based on ideological concepts but on her sense of physical reality. Toyo Ito described it like this: "The freedom and happiness that Sejima embraces, liberated from social conventions and restrictions, give her a greater insight into social realities. Unlike other architects, forced to comply with their chosen ideology, her process of visualizing her architecture is not conceptual. It is the physical expression of a person who responds freely to reality. She offers a non-judgmental critique and, in doing so, risks being misunderstood. In contemporary society, where ideology has been emptied of value, such physical acts, which visualize reality in a perfectly straightforward way, gain maximum critical power."[2]

Ito's "wind-like" weightlessness is expressed as forms. Sejima did not inherit that ideological, utopian approach from Ito, but learned the way he used materials and structures to achieve weightlessness. She builds objects by focusing on reality and creates programs based on realistic research into how the building will be used. However, she slightly shifts her conclusions after accumulating research. Then she lets her ideas lie fallow, while she explores two unknown variables: how the building will change the people who use it, and how the building will be changed by its users.

Sejima says that architecture is software as well as hardware. When the emphasis is placed on its character as software, as in the case of unintentional situations, "architecture creates a bridge between hardware and software." In other words, it deconstructs the border separating hardware from software. Naturally, it is difficult to clearly describe this delicate, undefined process. In this essay, I would like to discuss the development of this process in the following four chapters: Kazuyo Sejima's early works; the work of the SANAA studio since 1995; the partners' architectural philosophy through one of their most representative works, the 21st Century Museum of Contemporary Art in Kanazawa; their recent works.

Early Works–1995: The Quest for a New Architectural Language
In 1988, Kazuyo Sejima left Toyo Ito's office. Her first work as an independent architect, Platform, was critiqued with the adjective "light." This was not what she intended, however, since it clearly cut loose from all conventional architectural ideas. The title "Platform" was given to this private home, inspired by the platforms in a train station. Underlying it was the concept of a "platform" or a "stage," where various private lives unfold. The architecture embodies a number of devices designed to display the various acts performed inside a house so they are visible outside. The functions explored inside the structure are directly reflected outside in the design of the architecture. The creation of this direct relationship between interior and exterior has been her signature style ever since.

Sejima acknowledges she took Ito's criteria as the standard for her critique of her own works when she first become an independent architect. She inherited Ito's style, which has been described as cinematic and ephemeral, while creating her own forms. In order to understand Sejima's "lightness" and her idea of the "relationship between the human body and architecture," it will prove useful to examine Ito's architectural concepts. Ito uses images of moving architecture in the electronic age. Like Mies van der Rohe's, Ito's architecture is an expression of ideas, the act of giving architectural form to his conceptions.

Instead of evoking images such as box, tent or hut, Ito's architecture contrasts weight and lightness, container and contained, contraction and dilatation, transparency and opaqueness, and explores the contrasts between different paradigms. In other words, Ito's buildings express both gravity and antigravity; they also seek to go beyond the concept of enclosure, which has always been an objective in architecture. As Koolhaas notes, the reality of Ito's architecture "not only floats lightly but also comes closer and closer to our senses." It is based on the dualism of our physicality, which Ito analyzes. Our bodies are combinations of a primitive physical body and another body with a high information content which exists in a virtual space created by information. Ito's architectural space accepts this dualism.

In contrast with Ito's conceptual interpretation, derived from his ideas about the human body, Sejima adopts a more practical approach, extracting her ideas from the accumulation of her own physical experiences. Sejima's rapport with physical space is detached from any historical context; but it seeks equally and ultimately to cleave to reality through an open, defenseless attitude. The distinctive feature of Platform is that it includes variously designed functional zones in a large living space: in fact it looks rather like one of Ito's architectural works. However, when we look at its "stage quality," which was a priority, we can see that everything else is balanced to suit to that priority. As a result the architecture appears to be "light," but not ephemeral. This ephemeral quality, intended in theory, is an anti-concept, being opposed to the ideology of permanent architecture. Sejima, unshackled by any ideology, considers durability merely a parameter agreed on with her client.

One of the elements Sejima sees as important in designing a structure is what people do in the building and how they use it. She focuses on the "temporal sequence": actions and events caused by living in that building. When the movements of the people inside the building are visible from without, the sequence of events becomes a part of its external appearance. The way she looks at events reflects how she perceives contemporary situations.

Sejima proceeds by trial and error in making decisions about her agenda. Her working method has been called "diagram architecture," a process that evolves around two-dimensional plans followed by three-dimensional models. She works by making countless plans and models created for study. Elevations and façades are left to the very last moment.

Her next project was Saishunkan Seiyaku Women's Dormitory (1990–91). Here Sejima's ideas entered their next experimental phase. It was built as a dormitory where eighty new female employees live together for one year in their training period. What was required was not to create an ideal space for individuals but one that would maximize the advantages of living together. Two buildings were erected on the 25 × 50 meter lot to accommodate eighty people. Between the two buildings Sejima placed a common room for use by all the residents and added terraces on both sides of the building. The large common room, which comprises the entrance space, hall, and bathrooms leads to the guestrooms, sitting rooms, and an office for maintenance staff. Sejima essentially divided the building into private rooms for four women with the minimum facilities and large public spaces.[3] The space is laid out as functions and positions. Does it create a spatial and relational conventional hierarchy between different functions? Can we find relations between divided functions? Is each function divided appropriately? Use different qualities in space for different functions?

For example, if a bedroom and living room and other shared spaces are arranged in a line, people's movements are restricted and a hierarchy is created. If the number of functional units is increased, the structure becomes too complex, with mutual relationships and differences in qualities. So Sejima placed different functional units in equivalent positions in the plan of the building. The distances between functions are sufficient for something else to have a chance to be placed between them, so that the relationships between the functions are not rigid. Her production notes show one direction she chose after these studies: a new line of thinking that led her away from conventional approaches to architecture. She considered the living space that integrates the whole as "outside." This perspective led to her later ideas: treating the buffer zone as a semi-outdoors. This buffer zone is still protected as part of the interior but it looks out on the landscape and lets in stimuli from outside.

21st Century Museum
of Contemporary Art, Kanazawa,
Japan 1999–2004
(Walter Niedermayr / Courtesy
Gallery Koyanagi, Tokyo).

As well as the contrast between shared spaces and private rooms, she established the contrasts of inside, buffer zone, and outside. This idea deconstructs the conventional idea of borders between private and public domains. Sejima looks critically at concepts such as personal space, identity, society, and public, which are not really clear, especially in Japan.

Though this building was criticized for degrading individuality and described as "jail-like," it seems to be the direct result of a program to correct the individualism that has gone too far in asserting personal freedom and private relationships against citizens' responsibility to the public. Architect Riken Yamamoto assessed Saishunkan Seiyaku Women's Dormitory as a radical approach to realizing the brief in a direct, physical way. Then he said this order is now reversed: the architecture forms the brief. Architecture leads programs.[4] This is a rehabilitation program for twenty-first century citizens that goes well beyond the intentions of her client.

Sejima's tendency to treat the whole space as a functional unit has been constant in her work ever since. Everything in this universe contains another small universe within it, and all the universes are equal. Her approach has a lot in common with holographic paradigms and a Shinto-like worldview: the part is a whole and the whole is a part. The whole is considered to be one function; it encourages and promotes mingling, causing unexpected encounters and reactions. This is exactly what we find in chaos theory. Sejima's architecture is designed with a minimal constructive order and system so as to foster unexpected movements.

Her approach is very remote from Western concepts, where value is identified with power, or twentieth-century modernism and individualism. Sejima's work appears to deconstruct modern architecture; but actually it originates from an absolutely different place. There is no frame of reference, and her handling of form is extremely simple and clear.

"Architectural design can only proceed through forms. Making architecture, if we can say this without fear of being misunderstood, is surely a question of creating new forms. This does not mean creating irregular forms or eccentric external forms. Working through sketches, our approach has always been based on the desire to create a new form that arises directly out of the architectural design. Designs are recognized by their forms, and moreover, the public or social aspect of architecture resides precisely in an understanding of the architecture and its relations to the structures surrounding it."[5]

There is another interesting episode that explains the logic in the way she separates various functions. For example, she made the radical decision to place the lavatories in the core pillar, which can be described as a "toilet tower." Lavatories, in general, are designed to be together at the back of a building. Sejima explained, "I didn't like the idea of everyone getting up and walking to the same place (lavatories) in the morning." This is one of her subconscious choreographies. She designs buildings so that people walk in unconventional flow lines. Through these random elements, she creates private times and spaces, which would have been impossible in an ordinary group residency. It is reminiscent of random coefficients in computer theory and agent theory, where programs are created without any central orders.

Sejima's work does not require theories based on a traditional context; various aspects of her theories are formed freely on the construction site. In the Saishunkan Seiyaku Dormitory she presented the new idea of limiting the individual, private space only to sleeping, while all the other human actions were designed to take place in buffer zones where personal and public life mingled.

SANAA 1995–2003: Architecture that Leads Programs

After the Saishunkan project, Ryue Nishizawa and Kazuyo Sejima together founded a studio called SANAA. Some of the new features they designed for the Multimedia Studio at Oogaki (Gifu prefecture) later became characteristic of SANAA. They harmonized it with its setting by designing a space that functions as a studio and gallery on a large site. The studio is 5 meters high. To keep the balance with the setting, the structure was built in the 1.8 meter hollow in the terrain. You can enter the building through the slightly curved roof. The metalworking and woodworking shops are surrounded by corridors, and jut out at the sides, rather like hernias. The gallery and three studios are divided by a courtyard, while the rooms are divided by functions, but one can walk easily and freely between them.

The Multimedia Studio has a large screen set at the end of the property. This is a flat open space that can be used for events and film productions. The corridors and courtyard are designed to connect each room to the exterior and one another.

The line of circulation through the building from the roof to downstairs makes a multilayered flow through the space possible. One experiences new perspectives walking down from the roof. The feeling as you go down to the studio is not of reaching some destination, but of walking through successive passageways and opening doors when necessary. The impression you get is of continuous lines of flow.

The same features appear in the apartment building at Kitagata (Gifu prefecture). The structure is just as thick as one side of an apartment; hence the very thin, ten-story building zig-zags along the streetfront outside the apartment site. The first floor is an open parking space under the building. It is designed so you can walk into the apartment lot from all directions. One hundred and seven apartments are encased in it from the second to the eleventh floors. Different layouts and types of apartments, such as one laid out on two floors with a stairwell, are combined in the building, so that its surface takes on various forms. The thin building, avoiding volume, is a fairly common form for collective housing. The one hundred and seven terraces open up the back of the building and make it less oppressive. It is designed to give direct access to the outside, so that people who live on the higher levels can still enjoy the weather and get some fresh air outside.

The stairs and corridors are designed so that all the apartments seem to be freely connected. From the terraces, residents can see people walking along the corridors and up the stairs. Each apartment consists of a terrace, dining kitchen, and bedroom. All of them are designed to receive sunlight and are connected by the sunroom and terrace space, which function as a buffer zone between exterior and interior. The south elevation is designed to show people moving through the building like figures on a screen. This reduced depth and direct encounter with the exterior were previously

used in her earlier work, Platform. The design deconstructs conventional ideas about private space.

Their designs of private homes show clearly how radical SANAA's ideas are. The way architects design residential spaces reflect how they see our time and situation. Social structures and people's psychologies have become much more varied; there is a marked gap between the way we live today and the way of life embodied in any conventional architectural vocabulary. Private housing is a good example. Conventional prototypes of human relationships, such as "happy families" and "individual private spaces," have begun to fall apart. SANAA questions the typical human relations upon which modern architectural formulas are based. Sejima proposes flexibility for residents in her apartment prototype for the Osaka Gas Showroom in 1991. She sets a kitchen and bathroom on either side of a cube-shaped room. The space in the middle is designed so it can be divided by movable container-partitions. The most fundamental needs, such as eating, excretion, and bathing, are considered first; then the two dimensional plan is laid out and the rest is left for the residents to design, as if the architect's work has nothing to do with the ethics and ideology of the residents. The architecture shows that lifestyles and human relationships are more diverse than ever. "This is also another example of the direction in which 'architecture leads programs'" (Yamamoto).

The architect Jun Aoki further explains that Sejima entertains different hypotheses about "the human behaviors which the built space is meant to house."[6] He stresses the differences between the Multimedia Studio and the N Museum. The intricate three-dimensional spatial structure and the distinctive spatial experiences fostered by the former disappear in the latter and the internal divisions are removed. Here the two architects have brought the architectural brief and built forms closer. Therefore, "the conventional, and easily grasped geometrical forms, such as parallelepipeds and cylinders are altogether replaced by shapeless forms without internal divisions. ... Instead of reducing spatial restrictions by creating a distance from human behavior, it uses human behavior observed from a distance."

In the N Museum, SANAA designed a look that displays "human behavior taking place in space," regardless of the architect's intentions. The N Museum houses permanent collections of work by two traditional Japanese artists as well as other collections and the usual facilities for visitors. The exhibition space is a large box in the center, surrounded by a corridor space where visitors can socialize. The structures containing the storage space, offices, and washrooms form two rectangular wings projecting in different directions from the corridor space. Although each function is clearly stated in the plan, the building itself and the two rectangular wings look like a single coherent volume when observed from different points of view. The gallery is set in the middle of the building. Visitors circulate through the surrounding space, which functions as a transitional area between interior and exterior. The building is low, so that it fits in with its surroundings, and it appears to have the same volume when viewed from any direction.

In the N Museum, the software called the "museum" is organized to provide a simple "exhibiting" function, and the architects' interpretation of the brief—the way the building is used—is still simple and "distant."

21st Century Museum of Contemporary Art, Kanazawa:
A Shared Vision for the Twenty-First Century

The 1999–2004 project for the 21st Century Museum of Contemporary Art in Kanazawa is a larger, more complex project and embodies a new approach to planning a museum. The museum possesses a remarkable gallery for displaying art as well as functioning as an art communication center with spaces that can be rented for other activities. Interpreting the brief meant deciding how to relate these two functions to each other.[7]

Nishizawa interprets this extraordinary space by creating elements of contrast and continuity between the architecture and its setting. It is not an isolated "world apart," but rather an extraordinary space that is so interactive that it transforms its setting seen through this space. Transparency has a special meaning in this museum. It is not just a way of achieving lightness, information, openness, and illumination, or including human movement as a part of the design, which has been Sejima's tendency ever since Platform. It is about "the feel of life."

We all have experienced that transparent fish and plants, or human veins seen through skin, all look stiff and opaque as soon as they cease living. Using transparency to evoke life and freshness succeeded in this museum. Why did it require such a feel of life? The answer was because this museum was planned to create two-way interactions of a kind appropriate to the twenty-first century instead of the one-way educational purpose typical of the nineteenth century. This philosophy of interaction and transparency were already characteristic of SANAA before they started work on the museum concept. This project was different from their previous ones, as SANAA themselves noted, in the sense that the curators gave them a very concrete, detailed brief. The points they stipulated were: the museum building should be flexible enough to display contemporary artworks which differ widely in size, materials and media, and should respect their independence; it should avoid the financial inefficiency of creating and destroying temporary walls for each exhibition; the galleries should basically have natural lighting, supplemented by artificial lighting; the inside of the building should look simple and restrained, with plant and equipment as unobtrusive as possible. Securing the independence of individual artworks and avoiding the mingling of sounds or smells is quite different from isolating artworks. These requirements naturally led to the following ideas: the need for independent galleries of different proportions and sizes; the corridors should be wide enough to transport artworks and also contain the public: i.e. the corridors should also be able to double as galleries; there should be no hierarchy between galleries and there should be an atmosphere that enables galleries with different characteristics to coexist; hence it should be possible to combine any of the galleries. Different exhibitions will run concurrently and audiences should be able to take different routes each time so as to experience the space differently; the independence of each gallery should allow the public to return to certain galleries of their choice. This can avoid the confusion and contamination of visual memory caused by being forced to view other artworks, which is often the case in museums consisting of series of large galleries set in sequence.

Many of these features are meant to give the audience the pleasure of wandering about freely, rather as if they were visiting someone else's house. This gives them an unconscious sense of independence.

Before going into the details of the building, I would like to discuss the museum concept a bit further, because it has a lot in common with SANAA's design philosophy. When, as curator, I planned the Istanbul Biennial exhibition in 2001, I presented the theme of deconstructing Western social processes. A major paradigm shift underlying this theme was expressed as "from 3Ms to 3Cs," meaning a paradigm shift from (individual) man, materialism and monetarism to coexistence, collective intelligence, and consciousness. The 3Cs embodied my idea of new wealth for a better life as well as a lifeline for survival.[8]

Cameras, video cameras, and personal computers linked in networks, all now widely available, can transform us from recipients of information to senders. By being skeptical of conventional values and accessing information provided by others we can form new relationships. New creations have become possible through synergy, though they were impossible when we were isolated and disconnected. In the twenty-first century, museums have to be aware of this shift in the "subject" and assist in accelerating it. Two-way communication became possible when people acquired the media that made them active subjects sending out messages. In other words, it is an authentic way to discover others. Horizontality without hierarchy, flexibility and transformation through interactive processes: these are the principal features of SANAA's museum project.

This museum is located in the center of a medium-sized city with a population of 450,000. It is surrounded by streets and a reservoir. SANAA planned to give the building a cylindrical form right from the start. That makes it equally accessible from all directions, without any distinction between front and back. The outer walls are made of glass, reflecting the surrounding landscape. It was designed so that the inside and outside of the building overlap visually in the curved glass surface. The galleries form the core, and ranged around them are the art communication facilities such as the library, conference room, theater, children's workshop room, cafeteria, and shop. Two zones, the museum zone (admission tickets are required) and the socializing zone (public area and free admission), are encased in one building. Those two zones are visually linked, divided only by transparent acrylic doors and the intervening courtyards. Except for the walls of the galleries, which exist as spatial volumes, there are no pillars, stairs or anything else of the sort to clutter the sightlines. The courtyards are immaterial spaces bathed in light. Visitors have the extraordinary experience of being exposed to natural light in the courtyards and the corridors, where it is shed through skylights in the ceilings between the galleries. At one point, the light is so bright that you need sunglasses, but by and large it achieves normal levels of natural lighting.

Rather like streets, some corridors traverse the building from north to south, and east to west, providing links with the landscapes outside. This unique spatial experience can be compared to walking through one of the cities described in Italo Calvino's *Invisible Cities*. Because the space is highly transparent and immaterial, the act of viewing becomes purified. What you do notice are the works of art, brightness, and also the public, rather as if the people were performing on a white stage. This museum space accepts not only the physical bodies of the visitors but also their information-rich bodies as they interpret and react emotively to the contents communicated by the artworks.

The average height of the ceilings is 4 meters. A large round roof, 110 meters across, spans the whole structure, with gallery volumes (hereafter called "boxes") jutting out at different heights and with different forms. The rooms necessary for the various activities are seen as they are, as part of the exterior of the building. Seen from outside the architecture looks lucid and rational. SANAA have succeeded in this difficult process of realizing their "sculptural" composition while adjusting to the requests from the curators to provide varied and dramatic viewing routes.

This extraordinarily weightless, immaterial-looking interior and exterior were achieved in collaboration with the structural engineer Mutsuro Sasaki. The important elements include a thin roof that eliminates any sense of heaviness in the exterior and slender pillars that avoid blocking the views. This type of structure would usually require 40 × 20-centimeter beams, but adopting synthetic beams made of a combination of steel grid, steel sheaths, and concrete enabled the beams to be pared down to 20 centimeters. The thin roof rests on slender pillars randomly placed around the socializing zone and the courtyards, as well as H-shaped steel pillars embedded in the walls of the gallery boxes. The pillars are steel cylinders and they come in three diameters (11, 9.5 and 8.5 centimeters) depending on the weight of the roof they have to support. The roof and the box walls are connected with 3-meter H-shaped steel grids.

Structural engineers used to be mainly responsible for ensuring projects were safe and on budget. Now, at the start of the twenty-first century, engineers play an important part in making the architect's free formation structurally possible as part of the creative effort directed toward collective intelligence and synergy.

The curators studied museums around the world to plan variations on gallery proportions. They had models made for study and selected fourteen different forms. They fixed on four ceiling heights of 3, 8, 6, 9, and 12 meters. The basic forms are square, the golden rectangle, and round. Though these rooms might not respond to all the needs of different artworks and exhibitions, still they felt that these variations would secure a maximum range to meet artists' intentions and needs. To decide on the final positioning and adjustments the curators worked together with SANAA and an intimate synergy resulted. It was SANAA's first experience of working to such a detailed brief and they turned out several hundred plans and models.

So the forms of the galleries were stipulated by the curators and created by the architects. I feel this idea was an extension the concept of flexibility SANAA had already developed. The flexibility to choose from galleries with set proportions is different from the kind of flexibility typical of Modernism, where a large room would be divided up freely. It fulfills the brief through collaboration between the designers of the rooms and the people who are going to use them. In contrast to Modernism's version of physical flexibility, this is enhanced by the effort of the designer to read the specifications supplied by the client and make the most of them.

If we suppose that any architectural structure can be used efficiently, provided the users are flexible enough, then ultimately architects and architectural programs are no longer needed. In other words, the concept of "architecture" itself disappears. In an interview with other architects, Kazuo Shinohara and Noriaki Okabe, Sejima gave full credit to the flexibility of users, but added: "Apart from spatial and physical flexibility,

there are invisible factors, such as information. These factors are creating situations that are totally different from in the past. So, I don't see any reason why architects have to try to create flexible architecture."[9]

It is as simple as this: people will react to any given restrictions. When questions arise, we naturally try to solve them. If our knowledge is insufficient, we use all our senses to respond. Since museums deal with fuzzy and ambiguous values (unlike schools and hospitals, which have fairly straightforward functions), they can clearly act as models for a "stimulating" space, one that continues to produce new programs on the basis of the users' responses.

This means that the "human behavior"(Aoki) envisioned in the brief should be considered as having an unpredictable, unlimited potential.

New Projects since 2004

Although new relationships between individuals and the whole or the public had already appeared in one form in the Saishunkan Seiyaku Women's Dormitory, the "whole" in this project had more the quality of a physical space. However, in the Kanazawa 21st Century Museum of Contemporary Art, the "whole" had more abstract qualities as a magnetic field of consciousness, a polyphonic place where different events can run and resonate concurrently. Since then, the area of the "new ego" as a metaphor has become both veiled and explicit. The creation of relationships with the environment and other people are continuously and concurrently reconsidered and reconstructed within SANAA. These propositions have been programmed and embodied in forms with various degrees of flexibility and strength in their recent works. They can be seen in the original forms of their large public facilities and in the interpretation of clients' briefs and one-off designs for private housing projects.

First of all I will discuss three museum projects still under way in 2005. One of them is the Glass Pavilion in the Toledo Museum of Art in Ohio. This is an annex for exhibiting glass collections; it includes a workshop. Rooms of different sizes with rounded corners are combined and enclosed in the square building. It looks rather like a steel lunch tray with lots of compartments or the inside of a spaceship. As seen in the plan, all the walls, except for six rooms (with white board walls) are made of glass. The space in between two glass walls functions as a buffer zone, controlling temperature and insulating noise. SANAA tried to express the visual concept of "transparency" through the smoothness of the curved glass surfaces and the multiplied effects of reflections. By clustering slender steel pillars all around the board walls, they maximize the look of glass as the main material and create gravitational illusions of glass walls supporting the roof. Here their main interest is to verify what it means to "experience glass," and they present this question to the visitors. The reflections always present overlapping images of the public and the interiors.

In the extension plan for the IVAM, the Institute of Modern Art in Valencia, SANAA boldly covered the existing building with a white mesh cube and used the space created between the building and envelope. It has been objected that this design masks the historical and social identity of the building. But the conventional representative conception of the façade was of no interest to SANAA. As they studied the environment their first concern was with the bright sunlight. Without changing the volume of the existing building, SANAA designed comfortable spaces for visitors, guided by keywords such as "skin" and "semi-outdoor space." The design created a new interface connecting the museum with its setting.

The design of the New Museum of Contemporary Art in downtown Manhattan was largely influenced by its location. The unusual structure of the seven-story building, which rises 53 meters high, was designed to secure high ceilings. Right in the middle of New York City, where many modern buildings are found, it stacks differently shaped rectangular boxes one on top of the other, staggering them slightly. The overlaps create space for terraces and skylights. This insecure, kinetically rhythmic form could be a critique of the city. The final challenge will be how to construct a visual critique of conventional relations in its vertical form.

The Learning Center at the EPFL (École Polytechnique Fédérale de Lausanne) should be mentioned as one of the studio's most important public projects. This is an experiment in how different programs can loosely relate to each other within a larger whole. The big, low rectangular building, measuring 175.5 × 121.5 meters, looks like a slight rise in the terrain. What is amazing about the plan is that all its functions, such as the hall, cafeteria, library, conference room, and study rooms, are housed in just one large room. The entrance is placed in the center so as to make it equidistant from each function and create smooth lines of flow. Furthermore the floor is elevated with an effect like a curtain being lifted to let the visitors in: people pass below the building to reach the entrance. (The height between the ground and the building varies from 0 to 7 meters). Visitors can enjoy views of Lake Leman from the highest point of the building. It can be seen as a variation on the Multimedia Studio in Gifu, where the entrance was set in the roof instead of under the floor, although the scales of the two buildings are completely incomparable. Various large courtyards, irregularly shaped and surrounded by glass walls, to divide the functions from each other. The light from the courtyards illuminates visitors passing under the building to reach the entrance. What they see above themselves through the glass is one of the functions they are now approaching.

Except for certain rooms with exceptionally high ceilings, such as the hall, the ceiling height is a steady 3.5 meters. As the floor rises, the ceiling also rises to keep the same height. Sejima says that if only the floor had sloped, it would have altered the proportions of the interior, which she wanted to avoid. "When the ceiling height changes along with the elevation of the floor, it changes spatial relationships and the sense of distance. For example, one can no longer see the mountains in the distance. It also makes it more apparent that ceilings and rooms are sometimes attached and detached by the shifts in the ceilings."[10]

The interior is basically one large space, though there are minor adjustments. For instance, the cellular offices and the partitions that rise to the ceilings were built to solve problems such as noise. Because the floor is laid out on different levels, some platforms had to be added to create an even surface on which to stand furniture. Unlike museums built to house artifacts, the Learning Center can take advantage of similarities between the programs whose main study is forms of human behavior. It can

immediately create a common magnetic field to foster unpredictable happenings in interactive relationships. Any inconveniences can be corrected locally.

Sejima's intention creates a certain distance between the separate functions and the whole, and careful adjustments in finalizing the design. Because of its irregular forms, three elements—courtyards, programmed spaces, and slopes of the floors—had to be organically related to each other. Sejima worked very closely with Sasaki, the structural engineer. Sasaki applied a sophisticated method using sensitivity analysis to design the freely curved surface of the shell. The architects kept feeding their ideal conditions into this program created by Sasaki and receiving feedback from it.

This organic form is related to its functions, which in turn inspire relationships and social behaviors. Because of the numerous variables, the elements generated by the architecture and the brief are equal and mutual: Yamamoto's principle, "Architecture leads programs," is not true here.

Nishizawa had always wanted to experiment with bold organic forms; however he claims he never had any big projects to realize them in. In this project he fused his direct approach toward the brief with the potential it offered.

Sejima and Nishizawa have different conceptions of form and they express this in their individual talents. We can see this in their separate projects. Sejima created a form for Onishi Civic Center by studying the relationship between the landscape setting and the building. Two of the three buildings have strange, rounded spoon-like forms projecting from the corners. Sejima conceived these forms through an intuitive reading of the context. Three buildings (gym, hall and foyer) had all to be related to each other. The three volumes had to appear to be one, creating smooth lines of flow. The inside should be visible from outside for security reasons. These elements led her to this form. The key term "indoor field," provided by the client, also inspired Sejima to create a variety of perspectives: the three buildings had to be visible from one another and the interior had to be visible from the exterior.

Sejima's drawings reflect the contrast between the clarity of the separate elements as she works to achieve a certain form and the unified final result, made possible by the technical precision of her structural engineer.

Nishizawa also designed an organic tear-drop form for the Naoshima Museum, which holds permanent exhibitions of two collections of artworks based on its theme of light. He created a huge undivided space by applying a large shell structure a using 22-centimeter concrete wall forming the shape of infinity. Because there are no edges, it is difficult to see where the exhibition space ends or judge the scale of the structure. Nishizawa tried to create an unusual setting, which includes nothing but light and works of art. This infinity wall was created as an experiment by the American artist James Turrell in his studio in the late 1960s. Turrell was interested in treating light as a physical material for his sculpture. The large-scale organic form also recalls one of Oscar Niemeyer's designs. This project by Nishizawa shows his interest in immaterial forms created by light and his urge to use light as an architectural material together with glass and concrete.

Another extraordinary Sejima work is the House Surrounded by Plum Trees built in Tokyo in 2001–03. This is a private home for five people of three different generations. The client wanted to keep the plum trees and link the rooms to form a single large unit. Sejima designed a small house with many rooms divided by thin steel walls (measuring 16 millimeters) with apertures of various forms without doors or glass panels. The result is each room is independent yet connected to form one large space. A child's room is divided into a bedroom and study. On the third floor there is a guest bedroom, a detached room, and a terrace room exclusively designed for activities such as sleeping and reading. These many rooms were designed for only five family members, so offering a variety of options. The purpose and use of each of the rooms can be swapped around freely according to the moods and needs of the family members.

Adjoining rooms, glimpses seen through the openings in the thin walls, look like paintings, losing the perspective of distance. People are always heard, but not necessarily seen. One room as small as the bed might seem a bit obsessive; however, the relationships created by the aperture in the wall create a spatial balance. This gentle territorial sense of individuality will certainly influence the children in establishing their identities. The little rooms are very flexible. For example, the wall dividing a child's room from the study could be removed in the future. Sejima created the project by adopting the key concept of "relating all the spaces in a unity" and responding to the client's personality. This is an extreme case of Sejima's readiness to pursue a statement to its critical edge. It shows how Sejima's architecture embodies her clients' values as well as its synergetic structure, including the time lag between creation and use.

Nishizawa's project for a private home, Moriyama House (completed in 2005), is an interesting example of the architect's interpretation of the client's brief. Here he was asked to design an apartment building that included the client's housing space. In response, Nishizawa separated the structure into five different-sized buildings. As seen in the plan, each building was given a separate entrance facing in different directions and a small garden. When the owner has collected enough rents from the tenants, each apartment space can be added to the owner's living space. Thus, Nishizawa designed a double-plan program of five apartments for five different families, which can eventually become parts of one large house. The invisible yet connecting lines of flow in the structure can also be closed down. This systematic and flexible plan provides a new relationship between tenants as well as between tenants and owner.

The Towada Museum project and its diagram with sixteen items inherits ideas from the 21st Century Museum of Contemporary Art in Kanazawa. It also explains the background concept of several buildings united in one property. This plan has a great deal in common with Moriyama House: the buildings are intended to have random and flexible relations with each other.

What is interesting is that Sejima's intuitive ideas always emerge from her anarchic physicality, unshackled by conventional notions, while Nishizawa's ideas have no existential perspectives based on his physicality. In other words, to Nishizawa, the environment, individual bodies, and buildings all have the same value. Ultimately, Sejima's approach starts from her inner self and attains a divine outlook, while Nishizawa's begins from a divine perspective and attains inner human perspectives.

Nishizawa's anarchic vision lies in his standardized, systematic worldview and is easier to understand within a logical framework. Consequently his vision appears less

exceptional than Sejima's. If we compare their collaborative projects with their individual works, we can clearly separate the independent contributions made by each architect and the results of their synergic fusion.

Conclusion

It is interesting to read an article from 2004 where Toyo Ito and photographer and publisher Yukio Futagawa discuss the 21st Century Museum of Contemporary Art in Kanazawa. They say it "lacks Sejima's signature style of physical sensibility" and does not have a mysterious feel of passion behind the abstraction.[11]

The reason why the architecture might have lost these elements is not clear. It might have happened in the process of realizing "friendly" attitudes toward artists and users, or through close synergic collaboration with museum staff members. However, Futagawa's regret and his sense of a "loss" in comparison with the talents of, say, Frank Gehry and Rem Koolhaas, is outdated, along with his concept of the architect's identity and individual style. In this case, SANAA only responded to presented conditions and realities, and simply became involved in and worked on the abstraction of the forms as they emerged through the process. They design not for private homeowners or corporate executives, but for the staff and public that will be using the building. They carefully created the programs for many more users than ever before. This was done under the common awareness of the paradigm shift from the "3Ms" to the "3Cs." They already had the talent to accept this synergy. The strongest talent is found in individuals who can listen to others, accept all they have to say, and create forms that still reveal their own styles, which are indelible, and certainly not among those who create only what they want to express. Forms distilled and enduring even when they have been sifted through the filters of synergy are truly strong and beautiful.

In the twenty-first century, architectural journals are not going to feature photos of immaculate, empty interiors or exteriors, elevations or isometric drawings; what they will show will be intelligent plans, statistics, research reports with diagrams, one photo of the exterior, and countless photos of the interior showing the well-used building filled with people. And they won't forget to attach a report showing how user-friendly buildings are. If it is a museum, the article should say what new high-quality site-specific artworks have been produced in the building. Features dealing with new architecture should be published at least one year after the "new" building has been completed.

Showcases displaying new physical forms of architecture will be outdated and useless. Architectural forms created to suit an ideological vision have had their day. The only survivors will be truly practical architects who will relate body and soul to the realities before them and realize buildings in forms with an almost acrobatic directness. This is because we live in an age where ideology no longer exists. Whether we like it or not, we live in an age where there's no room for ideology. From the Modernist's point of view, these twenty-first century architects seem "insane" or "mysterious." But isn't that the way people are?

That's how the "Wonderful Life" (described in the essay by the evolutionary biologist Stephen Jay Gould) occurred in the pre-Cambrian period; through an explosive emergence of countless unknown new species, followed by natural selection of the fittest. But it will be filtered through the stark facts of how architecture can be lived in and used by people, not through an ideological filter. At the beginning of twenty-second century, existing architectures will be divided into two categories: ones that are used by people and ones that aren't. The only thing that will be asked of the former kind will be how they have touched and penetrated the users' consciousness.

[1] K. Sejima, *Sejima Kazuyo Dokuhon-1998*, interview with the architect, A.D.A. Edita, Tokyo 1998, p. 30.
[2] T. Ito, "Diagram architecture," *Kazuyo Sejima 1988–1996*, monographic issue of *El Croquis*, 77, 1996, pp. 22–23.
[3] "Sejima's Design Notes," *Shinkenchiku*, 10, 1991, p. 225.
[4] R. Yamamoto, "Architecture leads programs – about Saishunkan Seiyaku Women's Dormitory," *Shinkenchiku*, 10, 1991, p. 226.
[5] K. Sejima, "My Recent Projects," *Emerging Idioms*, monographic issue of *JA*, 2, 1992, p. 21.
[6] J. Aoki, "The Flexibility of Kazuyo Sejima," *Kazuyo Sejima/Kazuyo Sejima + Ryue Nishizawa*, monographic issue of *JA*, 35, 1999, p. 6.
[7] R. Nishizawa, *Sejima Kazuyo + Ryue Nishizawa Dokuhon-2005*, interview with the architects, A.D.A. Edita, Tokyo 2005, pp. 227–28.
[8] Y. Hasegawa, "Emergence from the Edge of Chaos," *Egofugal – 7th International Istanbul Biennale*, exhibition catalogue, Istanbul Foundation for Culture and Arts, Istanbul 2001, pp. 12–25.
[9] K. Sejima, "Discussion with Kazuo Shinohara and Noriaki Okabe," *The Kenchiku Gijutsu*, 4, 1997, p. 29.
[10] K. Sejima, R. Nishizawa, "Kazuyo Sejima + Ryue Nishizawa," interview with the architects, *GA Japan*, 73, 2005, pp. 16–21.
[11] K. Sejima, R. Nishizawa, "Discussion with Toyo Ito and Yukio Futagawa," *GA Japan*, 71, 2004, pp. 32–39.

SANAA [Kazuyo Sejima + Ryue Nishizawa]

O Museum

Nagano, Japan 1995–99

The Ogasawa Museum lies on the slope of a mountain. The site is an isolated plateau formerly occupied by a castle from the Muromachi period (1392–1573). All that remains is a Shoin, a writing-desk alcove that, together with the archeological area, is an important heritage site.

Its suspended volume, raised off the ground, helps the building fit in with its setting and ensures the historical remains are clearly visible. Raising the building off the ground also helps protect art works from rising damp. The delicate curve of the building follows the contours of the landscape and it gradually emerges as you draw closer to the museum. A square has been laid out below the building, and a ramp leads from it to the entrance. Inside, the large lobby has a large strip window that frames the façade of the surviving Shoin. This leads into a linear sequence of exhibition rooms and, beyond them, a service area with a panoramic view over the ancient valley below. The fenestration is designed to merge this historic landscape with the exhibition space.

View of the forecourt and detail of the silkscreen-printed curtain wall.

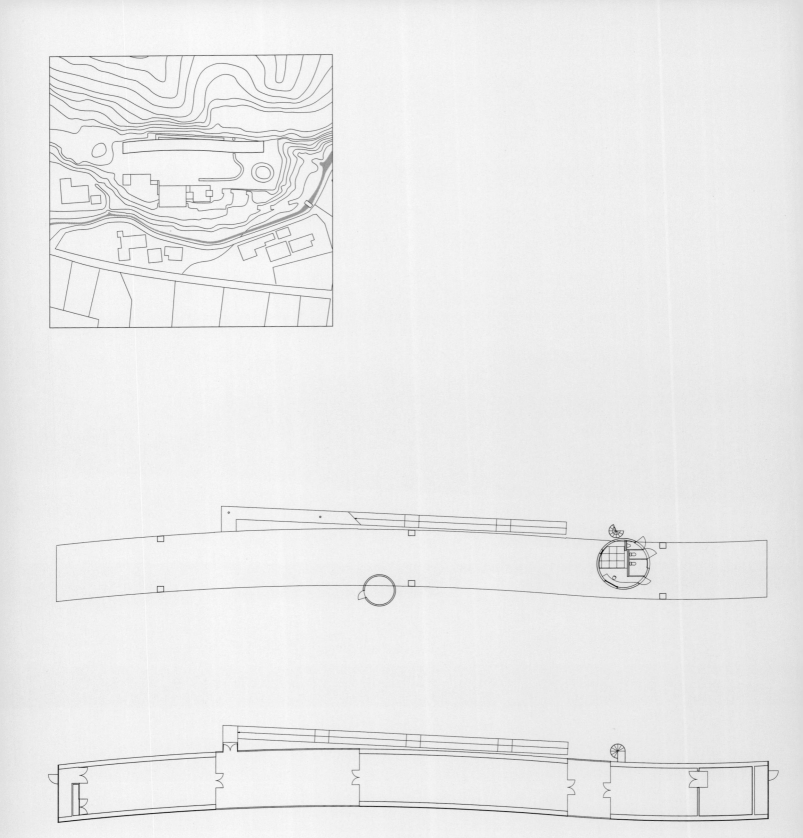

General layout and plans
of the first and second floors.
Southern elevation
and longitudinal section.

The portico beneath the building
and view of its sinusoidal form.

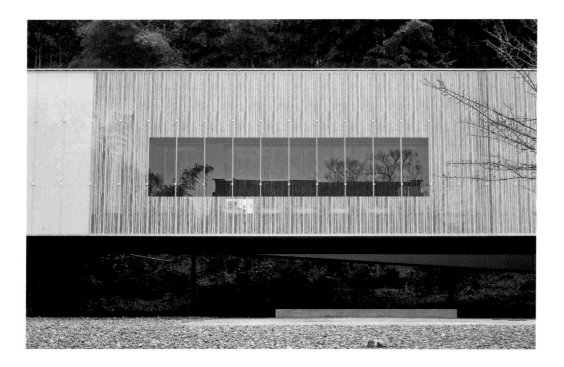

Nighttime and daytime views
of the entrance from the outside.

Front entrance at the summit
of the entry ramp.

Views of an exhibition room
and of the hall looking onto
the ancient Shoin.

N Museum
Wakayama, Japan 1995–97

The N Museum is a small building designed to house the works of two traditional Japanese painters. It stands in a tiny village on the banks of a river, nestling in the mountains of a nature reserve. For conservation reasons, the paintings had to be protected from natural light. Because of this, the exhibition spaces were concentrated in a concrete box that forms the core of the building. The windows that surround this elementary volume create a buffer space between interior and exterior and contain the washrooms, a loading area, storage area, and offices.

The site is flat and surrounded by mountains. It is equally accessible from all directions, so it was decided not to give the museum a clearly defined main façade. The plan is rather unusual and it is actually quite difficult to grasp the building's overall form. Through a special translucent film that covers the whole of the building's steel-and-glass envelope, the seasonal or daily variations in the weather and landscape alter the viewer's perception of the architecture. The black wall sometimes looks white or like a glass mirror or transparent, depending on the position of the sun. In the evening, the image of it as a continuous solid is dissolved and only the glass volumes can be seen.

View from the river and detail of the entrance on the west front.

Details of the envelope made of steel and glass panels.

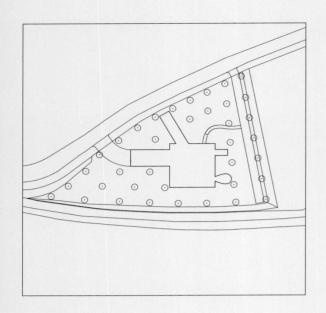

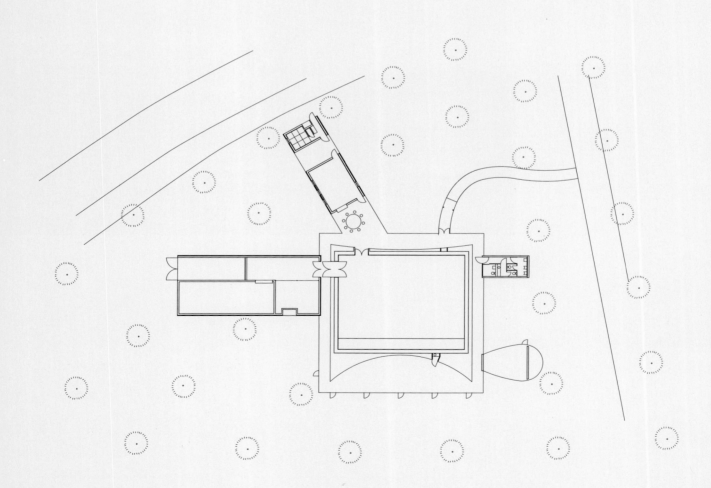

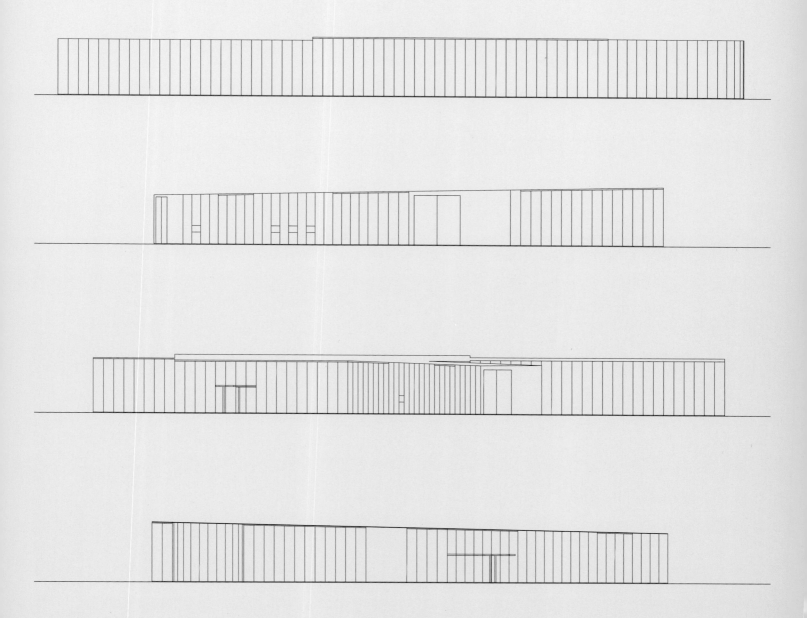

General layout and plan.

East, north, west, and south elevations.

Outside and inside details
of the distribution galleries
on the perimeter.

The open meeting space
for the public, looking onto
the river, and view of the central
exhibition room.

Park Café
Ibaraki, Japan 1997–98

This café is set in the middle of a large park, not far from Tokyo. The project sought to fuse interior and exterior. At the same time the building was planned to secure the smallest possible environmental impact. These objects were achieved by reducing the volume of the structural framework.

The effect the design sought was of an artificial forest beneath a slender roof, a natural shelter. The interior consists of numerous columns with slender profiles and four panels which secure the essential static and anti-seismic rigidity, sheathed in stainless steel with a mirror finish that reflects the surrounding landscape.

The furniture, both inside and out, has a similar finish and heightens the transparency and immateriality of the architecture by reflecting the nearby trees and the sky.

Nighttime and daytime views of the pavilion.

South view and an open end
of the building.

Detail of the pillars and
of the slender mirror-finish
load-bearing partitions.

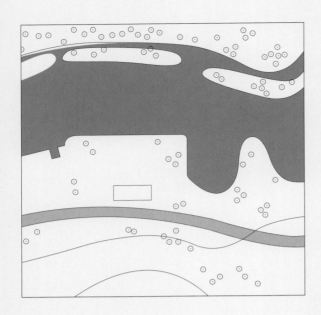

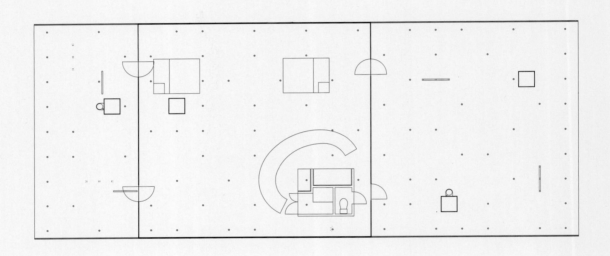

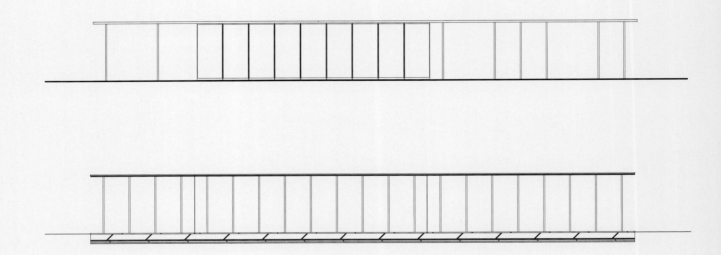

General layout and plan,
elevation and longitudinal section.

Constructional detail
of the section.

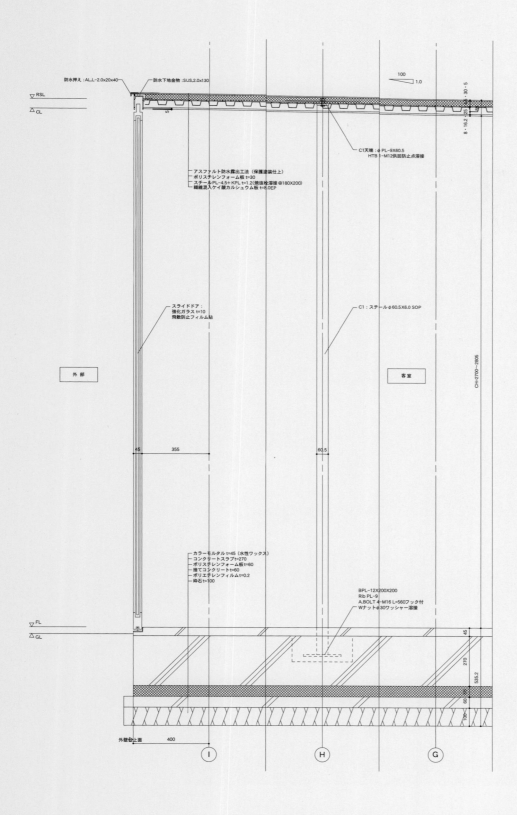

防水押え：AL.L-2.0x20x40   防水下地金物：SUS.2.0x130

▽ RSL
△ CL

100
1.0

C1天端：φPL-9X60.5
HTB 1-M12供回防止点溶接

アスファルト防水露出工法（保護塗装仕上）
ポリスチレンフォーム板 t=30
スチールPL-4.5+KPL t=1.2（焼抜栓溶接 @180X200）
繊維混入ケイ酸カルシュウム板 t=8.0EP

スライドドア：
強化ガラス t=10
飛散防止フィルム貼

C1：スチールφ60.5X6.0 SOP

外 部

客 室

CH=2700~2805

45   355

60.5

カラーモルタル t=45（水性ワックス）
コンクリートスラブ t=270
ポリスチレンフォーム板 t=60
捨コンクリート t=60
ポリエチレンフィルム t=0.2
砕石 t=100

BPL-12X200X200
Rib PL-9
A.BOLT 4-M16 L=560フック付
Wナットφ30ワッシャー溶接

▽ FL
△ GL

45
270
535.2
60

外壁仕上面   400

Ⓘ   Ⓗ   Ⓖ

63

Detail of the pattern silkscreen-printed on the mirror walls and views of the loggias.

De Kunstlinie Theater and Cultural Center
Almere, Holland 1998–present

Almere, a satellite town west of Amsterdam, is currently engaged carrying out important development projects. Under the master plan drafted by OMA, the SANAA firm was chosen to design the municipal theater and a cultural center on the lake facing the new urban center.

To foster interaction between professional artists and amateurs, it was decided to include the two functions within a single volume.

But the design makes the distinction explicit in the form of the building: it is expressed in its relation to both the built-up area of the new waterfront and to the horizontal surface of the artificial basin, on which the building will stand.

The plan of the complex is devoid of any hierarchy, with each spatial element, from the layout to the teaching rooms, given the same importance. This means that moving through the building is like moving through a series of rooms. But despite the apparent uniformity of the plan, the irregular expanse of the main floor creates areas which have different characters, influenced by changes in the way they relate to the water surrounding the building.

The load-bearing system and the partitions form a single system. The building's tough framework consists of flat steel uprights set inside what look like normal dividing walls.

The lake facing the new city center and view of the model from the east.

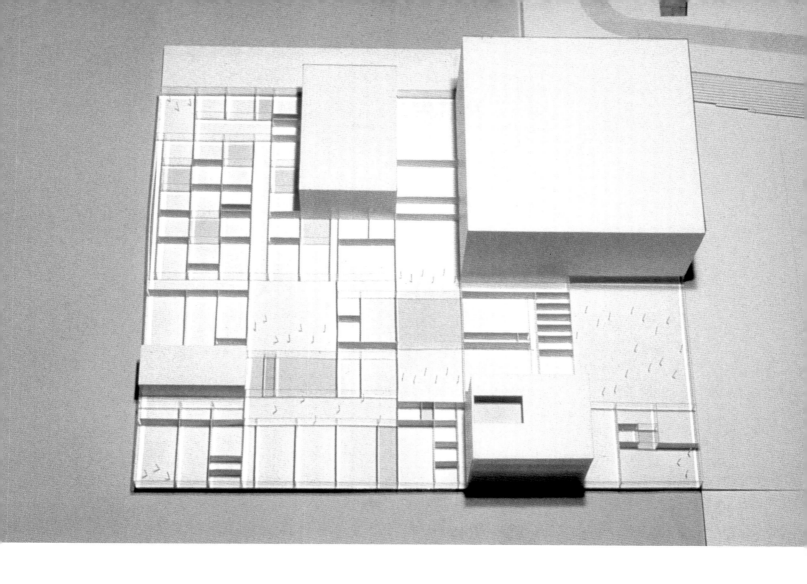

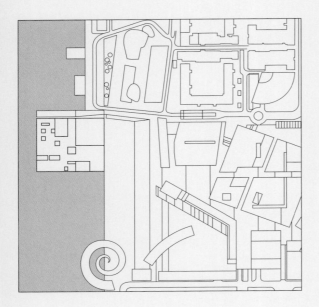

General layout and plan
of the first floor.

Views from south, west, east,
and north.

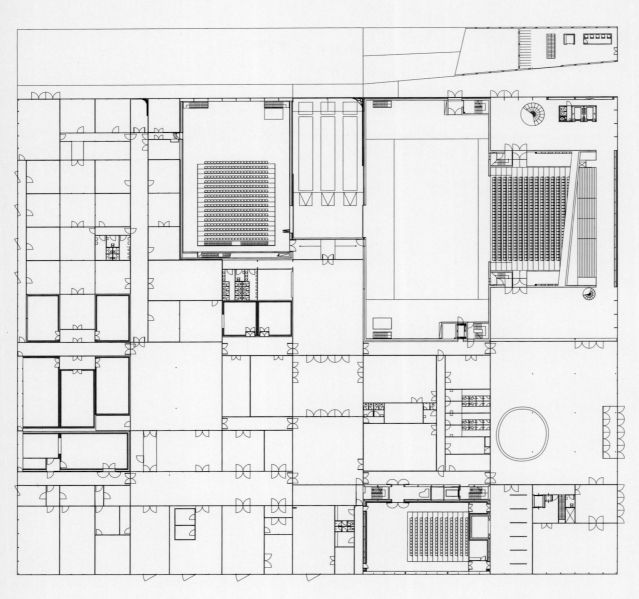

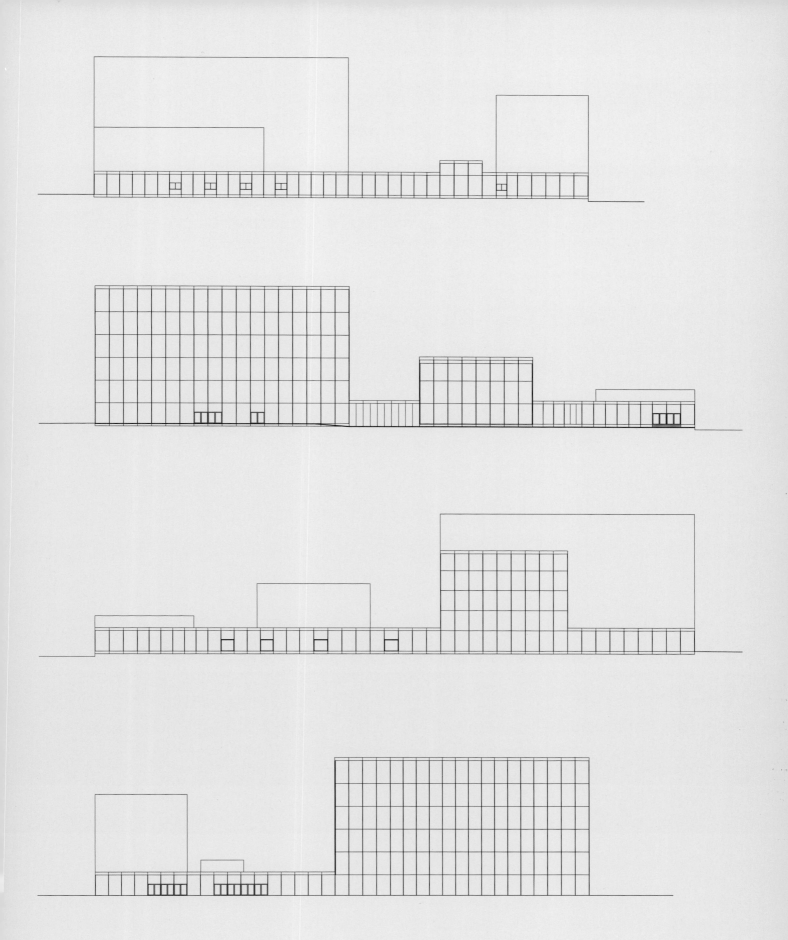

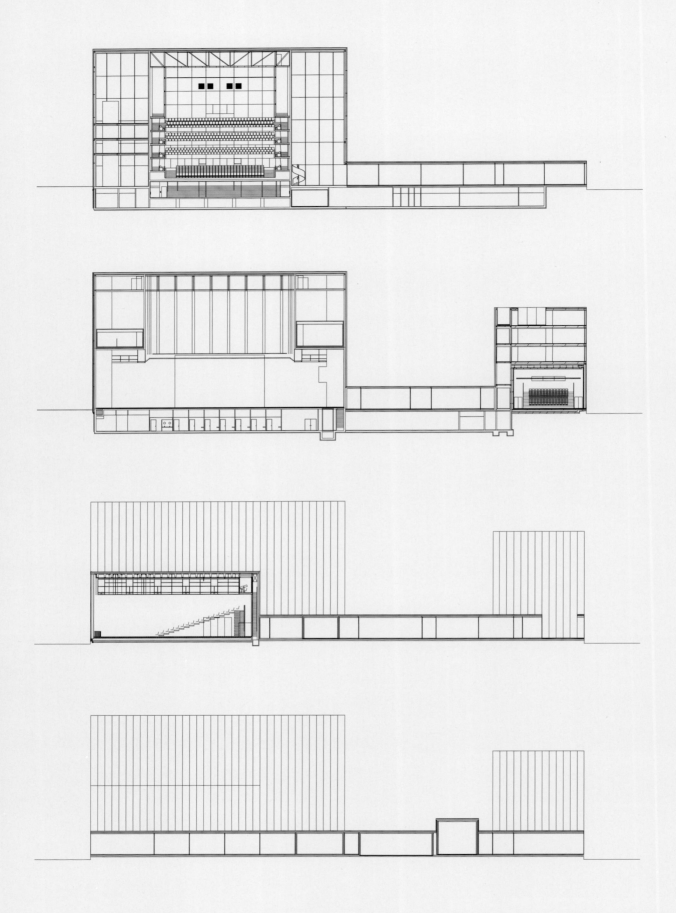

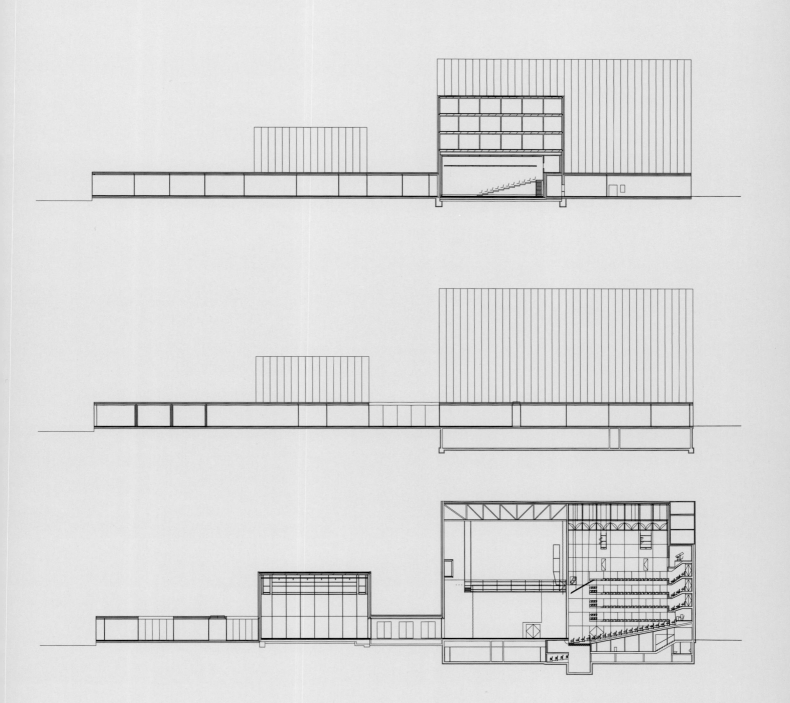

Cross sections of the large auditorium, the performance room, small auditorium, and music teaching rooms.

Cross sections.

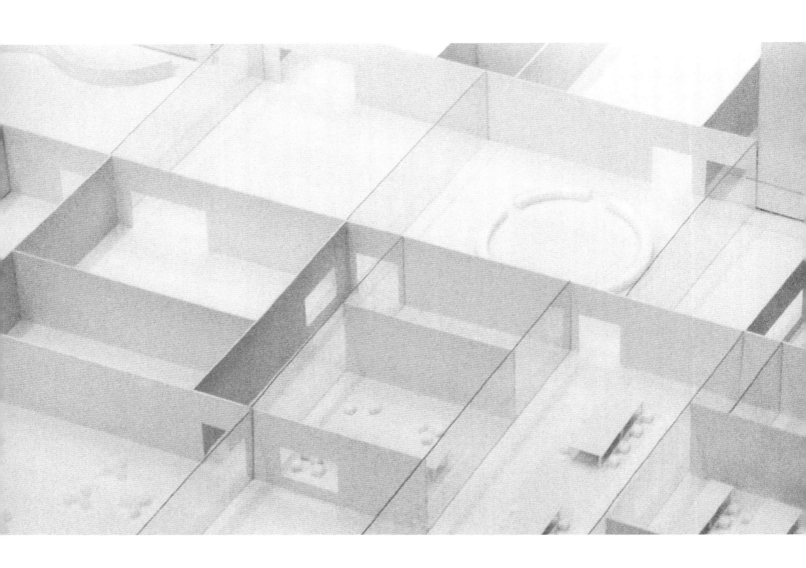

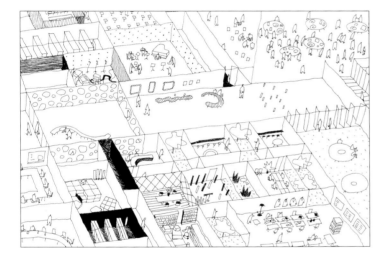

Detail of cross section
of the model.

Views of the entrance, patio-foyer,
and study sketch.

Views of the model: public foyer, the artists' foyer, small auditorium, and a music room.

The foyer of the studios for musical rehearsals.

21st Century Museum of Contemporary Art
Kanazawa, Ishikawa, Japan 1999–2004

The 21st Century Museum of Contemporary Art stands in the center of Kanazawa, a historic city of national importance on the north coast of Japan. Together with exhibition spaces, it houses municipal facilities such as a library, a conference room, and a workshop for children. The areas open to the general public and the museum facilities are designed to foster interaction between different groups of potential users, with the former laid out around the exhibition spaces.

The site connects the various public functions, all of equal importance, that surround it. Circular in form, the building has neither front nor back and can be viewed from all sides. The exhibition area is divided into a series of galleries embedded in a connective tissue of distribution routes. This arrangement makes it possible to use clusters of rooms having different features and at the same time define a flexible system of circulation that expands or contracts the zones with access by payment as required. The layout of the galleries creates transparency and a sense of openness, which is heightened by the long vistas extending through the whole building.

An ambulatory running round the inside of the curvilinear glass envelope offers a fascinating 360-degree view of the surroundings.

The exhibition spaces have different proportions and the illumination varies, ranging from the diffused light shed by skylights to rooms completely shielded from natural light. They vary in height from 4 to 12 meters. The sequences and finishes of the buffer zones are designed so they can be used as auxiliary exhibition spaces. Four inner courtyards, completely covered with glass, each with a distinctive design, bring abundant natural light into the core of the building and create a fluid boundary between the museum and the other public facilities. Despite its dimensions, the building is brightly lit, open, and versatile.

The museum in the urban context.

82

Views of the panoramic
ambulatory running round the
perimeter, and of an internal patio.

A corridor running through
the building.

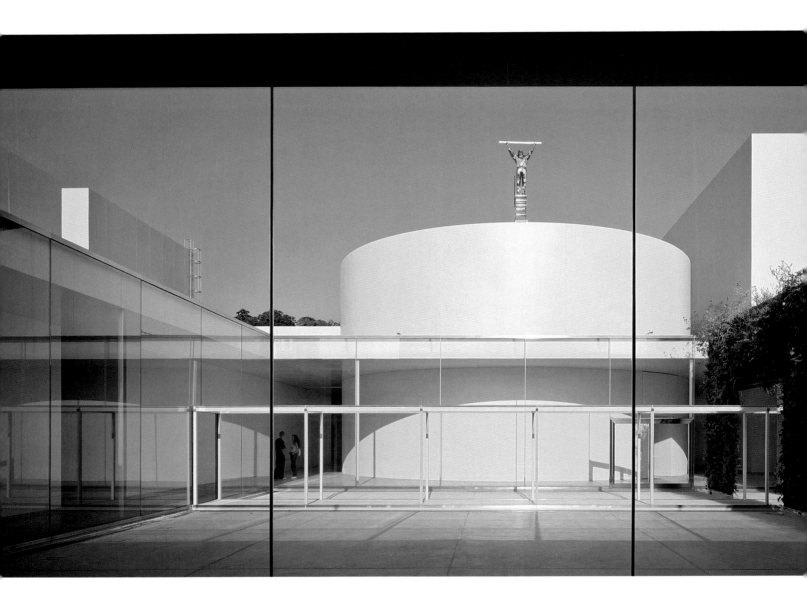

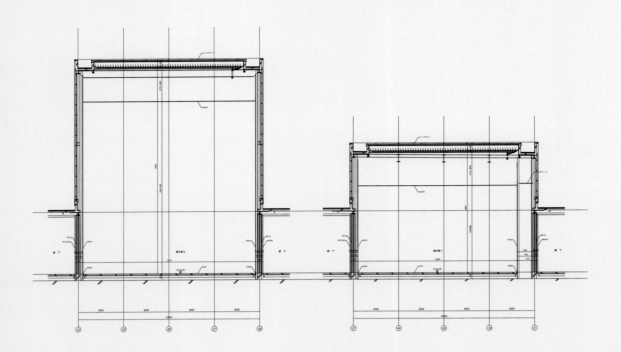

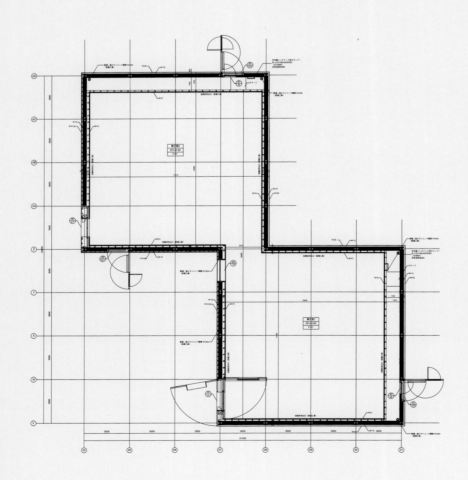

Sections and plans
of two exhibition rooms.

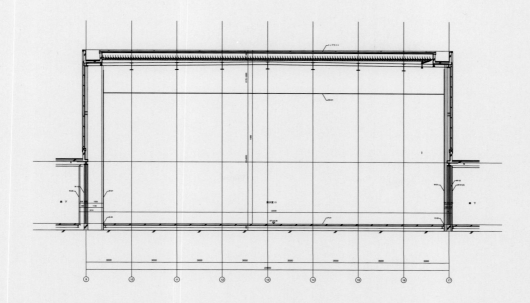

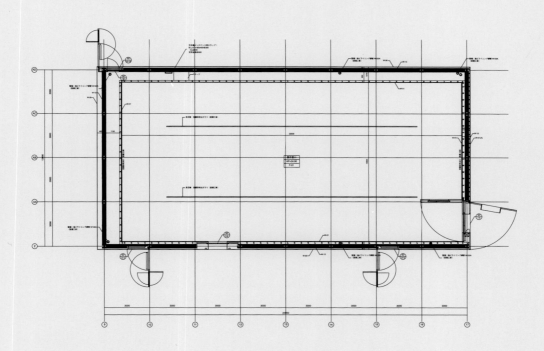

An exhibition room illuminated
by skylights and view
of the interior of the theater.

Dior Omotesando Store
Tokyo, Japan 2001–03

This flagship Christian Dior store is on Omotesando Avenue, Tokyo. The brief called for four retail floors and one multifunctional level, each laid out by a different designer. For this reason it was decided not to conceal the contents of the building behind an opaque façade, but of find ways to project the interiors of the building outside while creating a coherent, unified image.

The most significant feature of the site was the 5:1 ratio between the permitted height and the indoor surface area. So it was decided to make the most of the maximum height of 30 meters allowed by the local planning regulations to achieve the largest possible volume. This was then subdivided horizontally with separate floor and ceiling slabs, creating interiors that vary greatly in height, alternating retail spaces with the cavities used to house the utilities. This layered cross section creates the illusion it has more than just four floors, while keeping the interiors uncluttered. The building is completely transparent, being sheathed in flat panes of extra-clear glass. Behind these are curved translucent acrylic screens that provide glimpses of the sophisticated elegance of Dior's high fashion garments. The façade was meant to communicate the essence of the Dior style and, at the same time, eliminate the relationship between surface and volume customary in commercial spaces.

Entrance on Omotesando Avenue and nighttime view of the tower glowing in the urban landscape of Tokyo.

Detail of the façade with inter-floor
cavities of different heights
and view from the northwest.

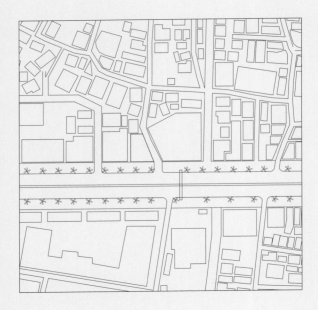

General layout, plan of the
standard floor and cross section.

Elevations on Omotesando
Avenue, and on the side,
rear, and east side streets.

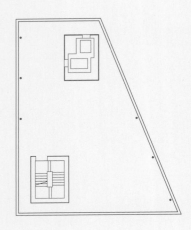

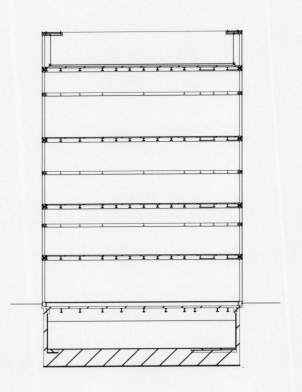

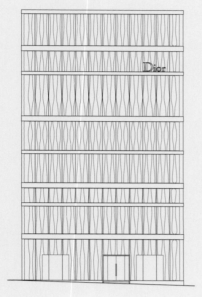

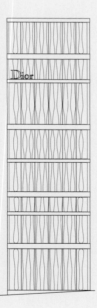

View and detail of the main front.

Details of the multilayered, translucent curtain wall.

View of a floor from the inside.

Detail of the screen draping made of acrylic panels.

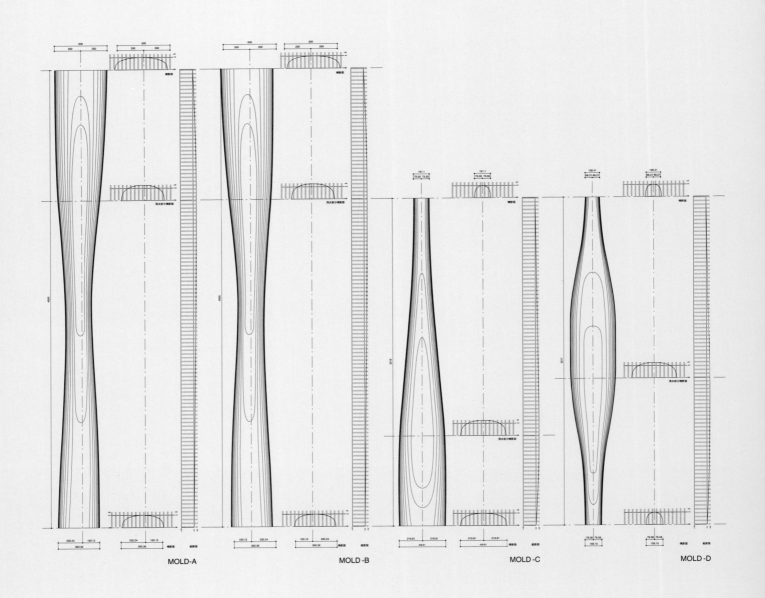

Working drawings of the curved
semitransparent acrylic panels
and phases of their production
using special templates.

MOLD-A   MOLD -B   MOLD -C   MOLD -D

Glass Pavilion at the Toledo Museum of Art

Toledo, Ohio, United States 2001–present

This addition to the Toledo Museum of Art houses an exhibition space for its collection of art glass and a laboratory for the production of the material. The pavilion is a volume laid out a single level, pierced by courtyards and visually permeable through various layers of transparent walls that give visitors a view of the surrounding vegetation at all times. Each space is enclosed within a crystal-clear glass envelope. This creates a system of buffer areas between the various units and provides insulation between the different microclimates in the exhibition rooms, the glass-making foundry, and the setting. The plan is based on a grid of rectangular shapes interlocking functionally, with curved glass surfaces linking one room to another. The walls enclosing the rooms form continuous glass planes without exposed corners. The public flows with the form through a sequence of interconnecting bubbles.

View of the building site
and full-scale model of the façade.

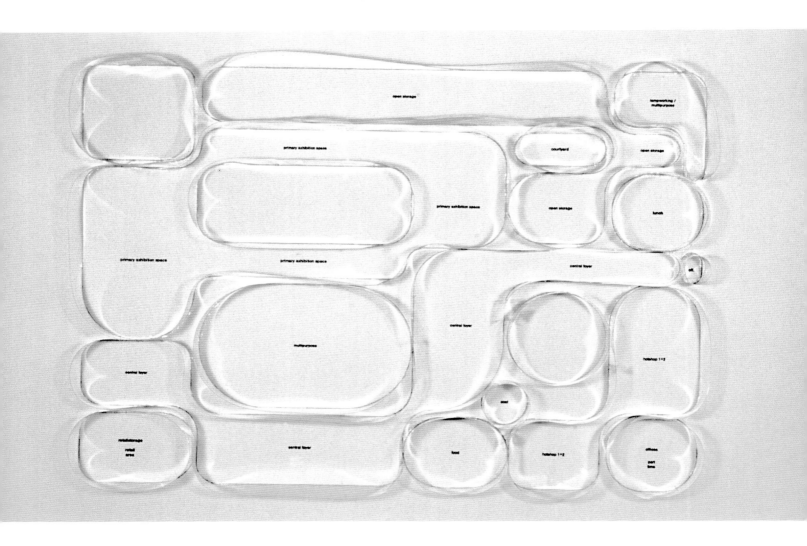

View from above of a study model and planning charts that show the conception of the plan, based on a modular grid of rectangular spatial cells with rounded edges and double glass envelope.

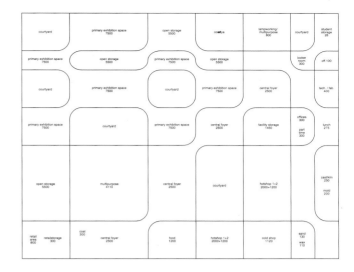

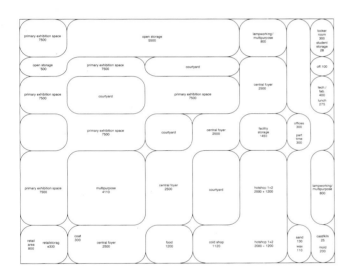

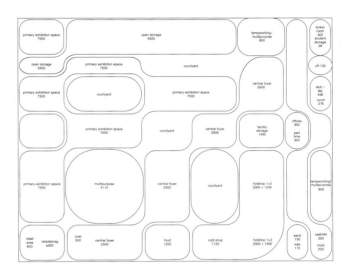

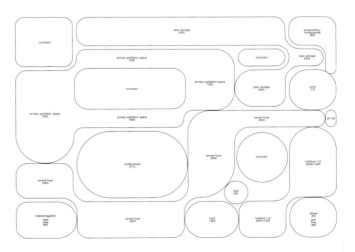

Detail of the façade and view from northwest.

Views inside the model.

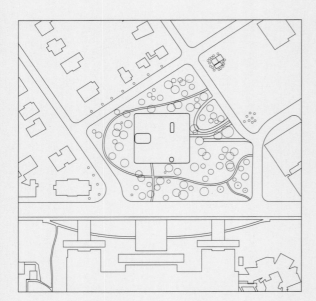

General layout and plan.

Longitudinal section and cross section, and northeast, southeast, northwest, and southwest elevations.

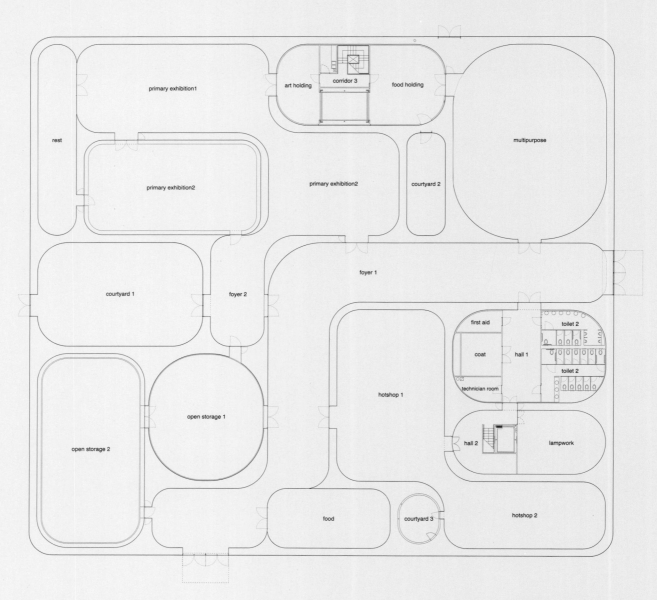

primary exhibition1

art holding

corridor 3

food holding

multipurpose

rest

primary exhibition2

primary exhibition2

courtyard 2

courtyard 1

foyer 2

foyer 1

first aid

toilet 2

coat

hall 1

hotshop 1

technician room

toilet 2

open storage 1

hall 2

lampwork

open storage 2

food

courtyard 3

hotshop 2

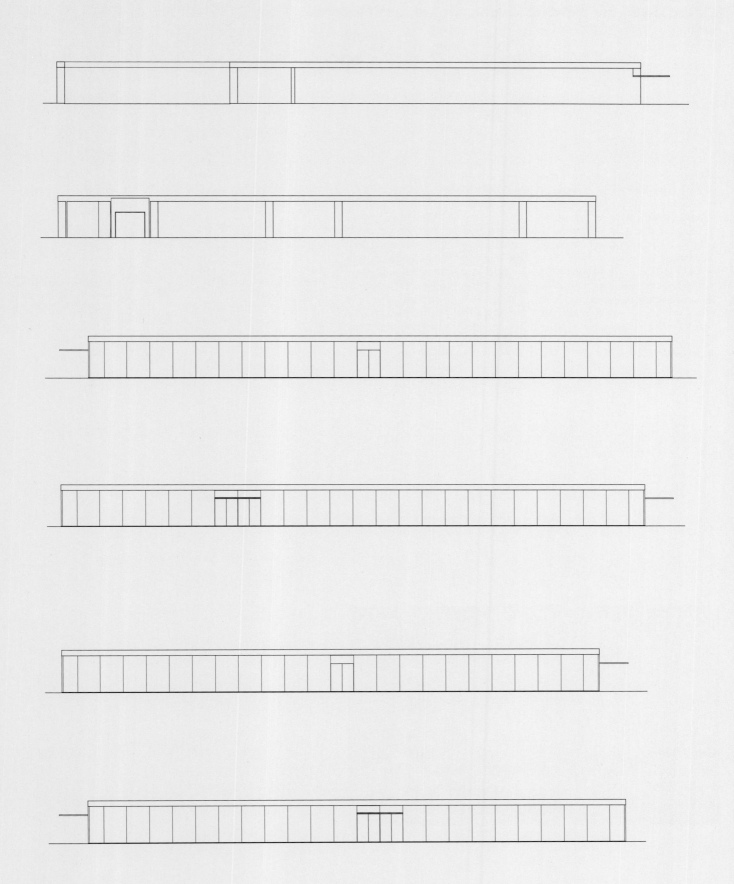

Extension to the Instituto Valenciano de Arte Moderno
Valencia, Spain 2002–present

The project is located on the edge of the old inner city. The complex of the Valencia Institute of Modern Art (IVAM) consists of an earlier museum building and a new office wing, both enclosed in a large permeable membrane of pierced steel. The metal envelope measures 90 × 90 meters and 33 meters high: it serves to screen out glare, wind, and rain. It creates a new semitransparent façade for the museum and also defines an intermediate space used for displaying sculptures with a roof terrace at the entrance that links all sides of the site.

Parts of this area, straddling interior and exterior, are climate-controlled by the geometry of the envelope and the flow of air conditioning from the museum. They can be used to supplement the museum facilities in the different seasons. The objective of the project was create a structure that filtered the light like the canopy of a forest and a space that would blur the distinction between interior and exterior.

Photomontage of the new volume on the building site; view inside the model level with the roof terrace.

114

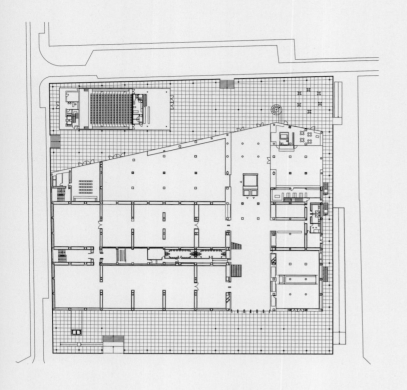

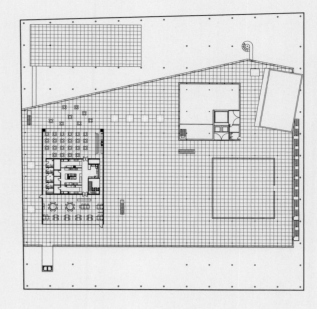

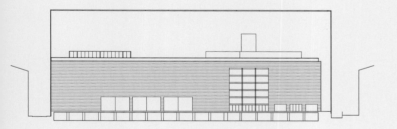

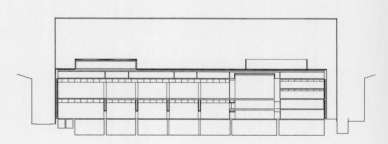

General layout and elevations:
south, north (Calle Na Jordana),
west (Calle Guillem de Castro),
and east (Calle Beneficencia).

Plans of the first floor,
on the level of the roof terrace,
and cross sections.

Views of the entrance
from Calle Guillem de Castro
and the space between
the street and the main front
of the existing building.

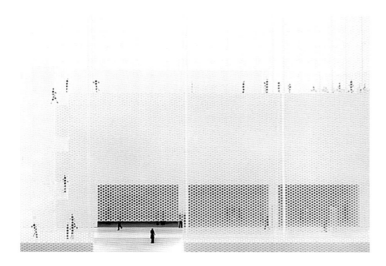

Views of the model.

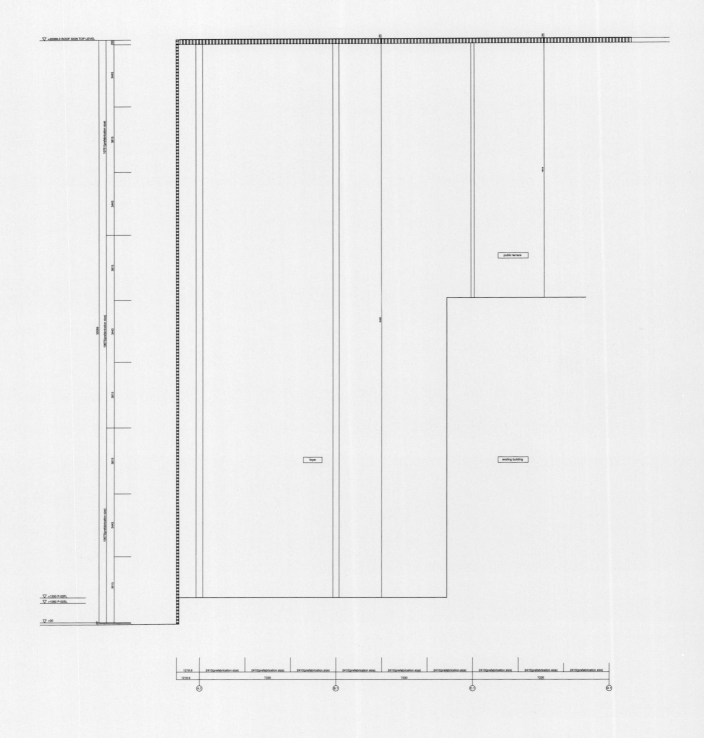

Detail of the cross section
of the façade and details
of the metal mesh used
for the envelope.

foyer

public terrace

existing building

Zollverein School of Design
Essen, Germany 2003–present

The Zollverein School of Design stands between an old carbon factory and a sprawling outer-city area. The building is a cube measuring 35 meters per side. It confronts the large scale of the industrial building and creates a marked contrast to the small-scale suburban fabric. With its substantial volume, it creates an entry to the former factory.

Judged by conventional standards the building might appear too wide for its functions. In actual fact the design not only aims to impose itself on the urban skyline but also fulfill a specific set of functions. The teaching spaces called for unusual heights, particularly in the common study area, which takes up a whole floor of the building.

This open-plan interior is a flexible space and unusually high, defined only by the supporting walls ranged around the perimeter. These walls, pierced with numerous apertures, filter the light and provide a view over the industrial landscape outside, easing the transition between interior and exterior.

Diagrams of the floor plans: first, second, third, and fourth.

Profile of the building and photomontage of the model on the site.

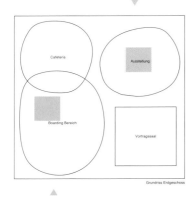

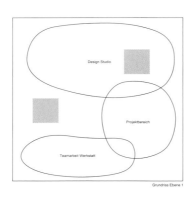

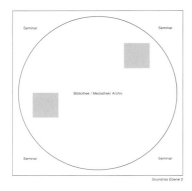

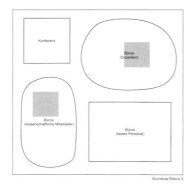

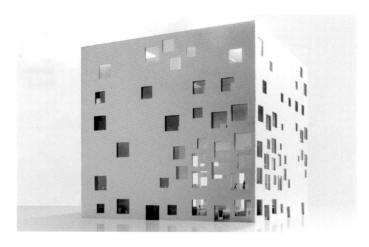

Detail and views of the interior
and exterior of the model.

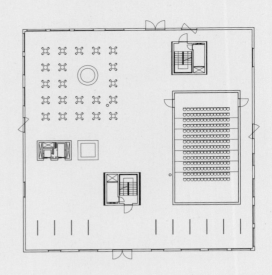

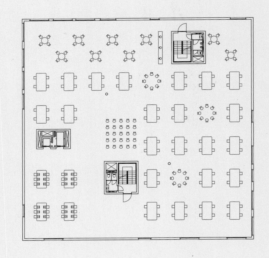

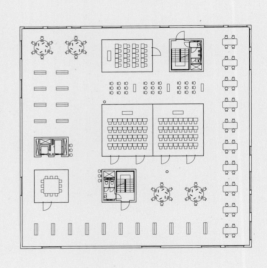

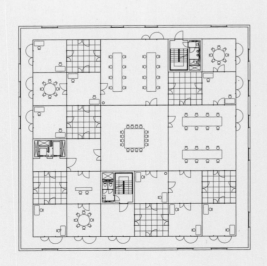

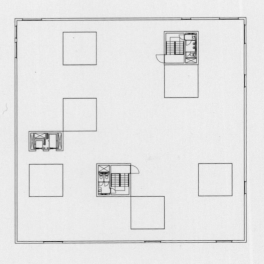

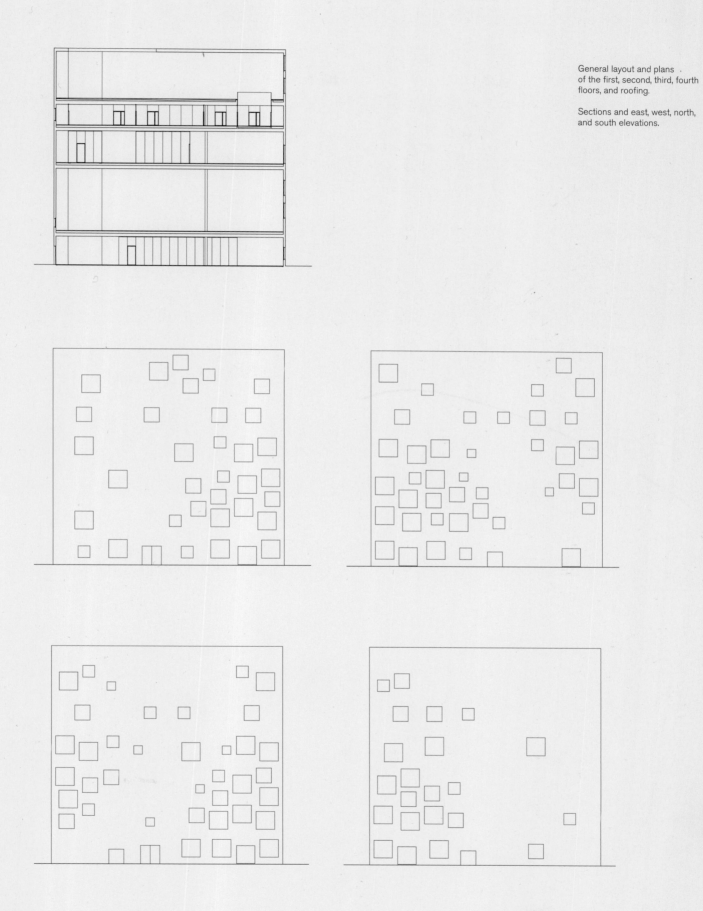

General layout and plans
of the first, second, third, fourth
floors, and roofing.

Sections and east, west, north,
and south elevations.

Views of the floor free for study, of the library, cafeteria, covered roof terrace, offices, and the auditorium.

128

New Museum of Contemporary Art
New York, United States, 2003–present

The New Museum of Contemporary Art is an architectural extension in the heart of Manhattan. In the congested urban fabric, the high-rise exhibition spaces could well have created a solid, introverted mass. But by staggering the different levels, the design opens up the building and relates the museum to its setting. The overlapping stories allow for the addition of skylights, terraces, and differentiated interiors, while increasing the amount of wall space and keeping the built volume within local planning limits. The changing relationship between the core containing the technical plant and the building's envelope also varies the amount and quality of the light shed inside it.

Details of the interior of the exhibition galleries and photomontage of the model seen from Prince Street.

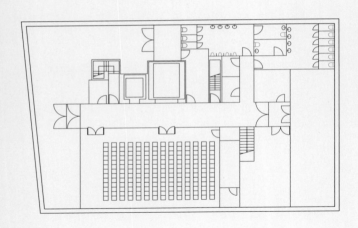

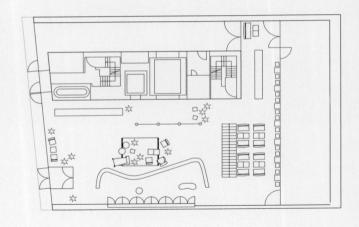

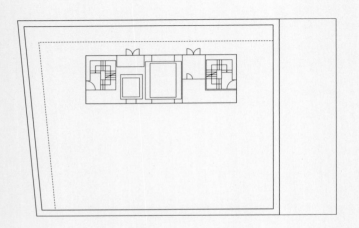

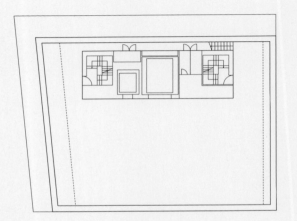

General layout and plans
of the first basement level
and the first, second, and
third floors.

Plans of the fourth, fifth, sixth,
and seventh floors.

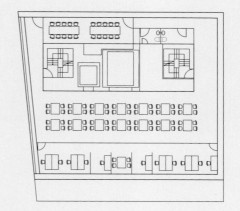

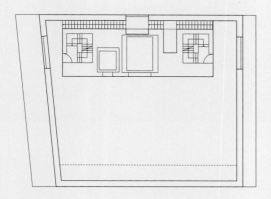

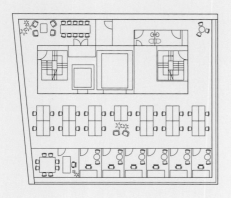

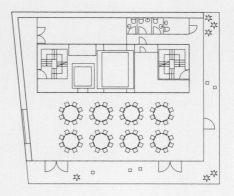

Photomontage of the project seen from the Bowery and study models.

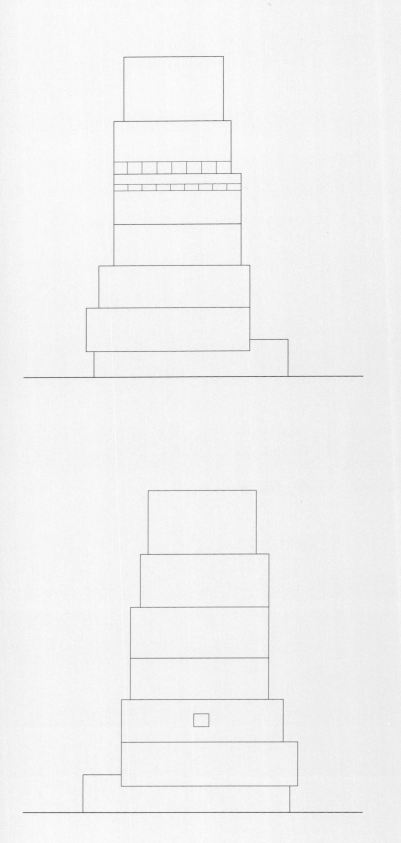

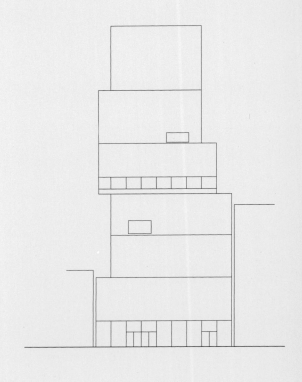

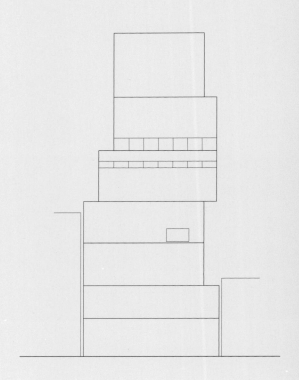

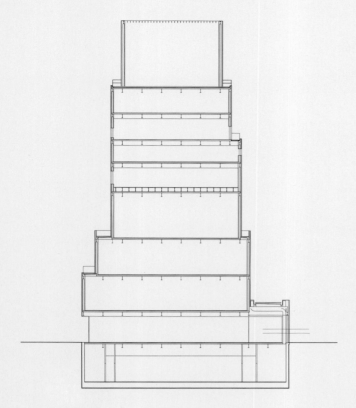

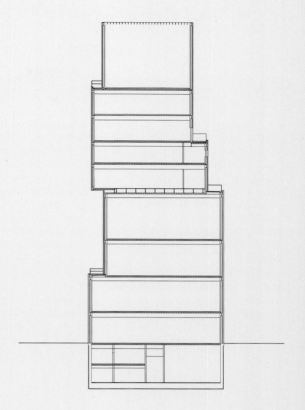

South, east, north, and west elevations.

Longitudinal section and cross section.

Novartis Office Building
Basel, Switzerland 2003–present

This building is part of the Novartis pharmaceutical group's new "campus." In addition to offices, it houses public facilities linked with the entrance to the campus, including a visitors' information bureau, coffee shop, and a branch bank. Its closeness to the gateway enables it to interact with both the business park and the city.

Company buildings generally have the vertical links and technical plant in the middle of the building and range the offices along the perimeter; but in this project both are positioned around the periphery of the building, enabling them to receive natural light and leaving space for a large courtyard in the middle of the block. This arrangement produces an open plan which is also discreetly articulated by the building's structural frame. The interior is not a sequence of private rooms, but it is not a typical open-plan layout either. The building is so narrow that the interiors seem to hover in the greenery of the park and passers-by on the street can see right through the building without much difficulty.

Full-scale model of the façade and detail of the study model.

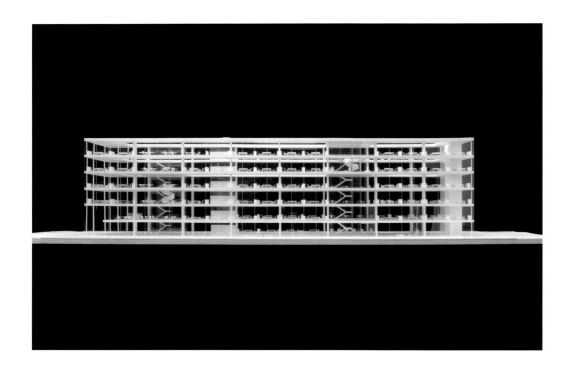

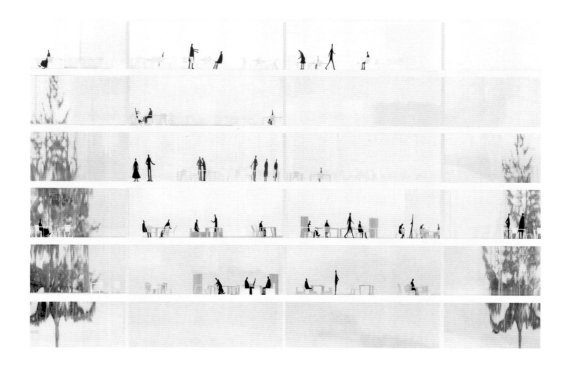

General view of the model
and drawing of a detail
of the front.

Detail of the model.

General layout and plan
of the standard floor.

Longitudinal section through
the patio, side elevation,
cross section, and front elevation.

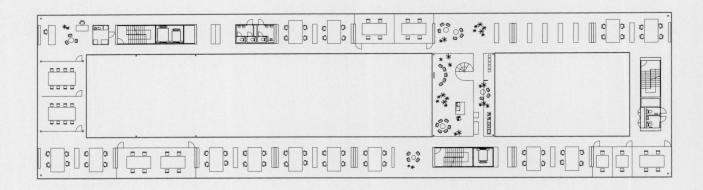

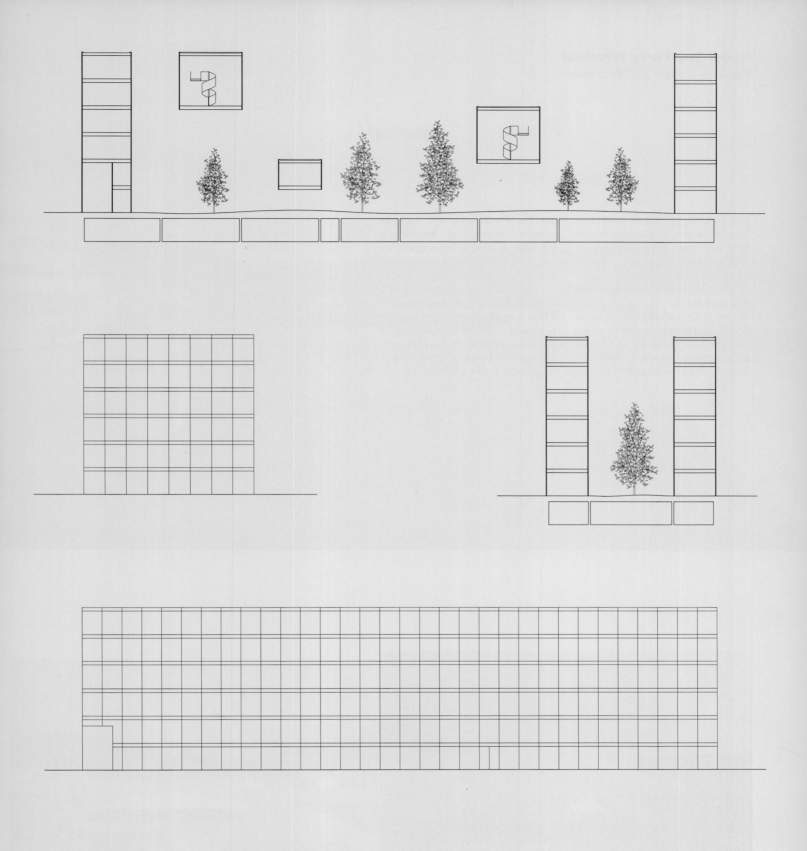

Learning Center of the École Polytechnique Fédérale de Lausanne
Lausanne, Switzerland 2005–present

The Learning Center of the École Polytechnique Fédérale de Lausanne (EPFL) is a multifunctional building containing a library, a center for the study of languages, offices, a cafeteria, restaurant, and lobby. This unified space set in the middle of its lot creates a point of social focus. The roof and floor have a slightly undulating form and are pierced by courtyards of different shapes and sizes. The main entrance can be approached from four sides by walking under the overhanging roof. Once inside, visitors traverse the gently undulating paving or pass beyond the patios and enter the various functional areas of the complex. From the slightly raised areas they can enjoy magnificent views of Lake Leman and the Alps beyond the campus.

The small courtyards and the variations in the height and breadth of the spaces create very different kinds of atmosphere. The seating in the multipurpose lobby can be extended across the artificial slope for important events. Students can read a book from the library sitting comfortably on a rise before the fine view or to drink coffee on a welcoming patio. The objective was create a place where the activities are separate but naturally related to each other, and create a single coherent setting.

Rendering set on the site and detail of the model exhibited at the 21st Century Museum of Contemporary Art, Kanazawa.

Elevation of the underground entrance area and general view of the model.

Details of the undulating form with a constant section.

Glimpses of the landscape
and the rooms above seen
from the undercroft.

Views of the interior of the model.

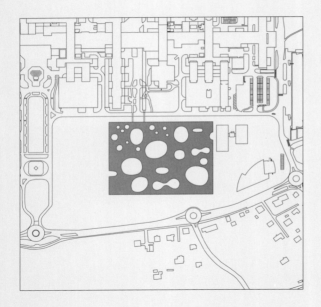

General layout, cross sections
and plan.

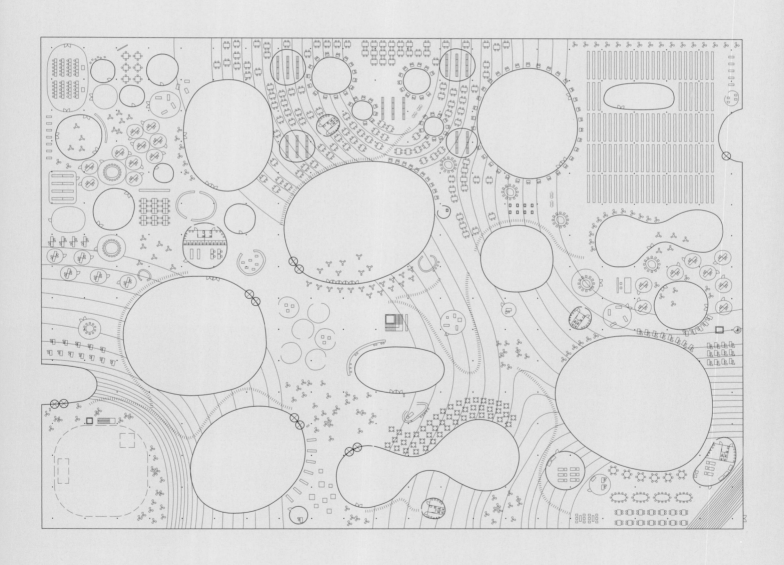

155

Kazuyo Sejima & Associates

Platform II Studio
Yamanashi, Japan 1988–90

This studio-home for a photographer stands on the slopes of Mount Yatsugatake and has a surface area of some 40 square meters. The lot backs onto a stand of trees, while the front overlooks tilled fields. The key to the design of this studio apartment was the use of natural lighting and the open layout of the living quarters. This was achieved by setting the various functional elements of the house on a sort of stage, an arrangement reflected in the form of the building. The different functions are positioned on the site, each assigned an area to itself defined by its structure and adapted to the terrain. The envelope covering the whole derives from the connection of these separate parts.

Detail of an entrance and view from northwest.

View of the interior, plan,
longitudinal section,
and west front.

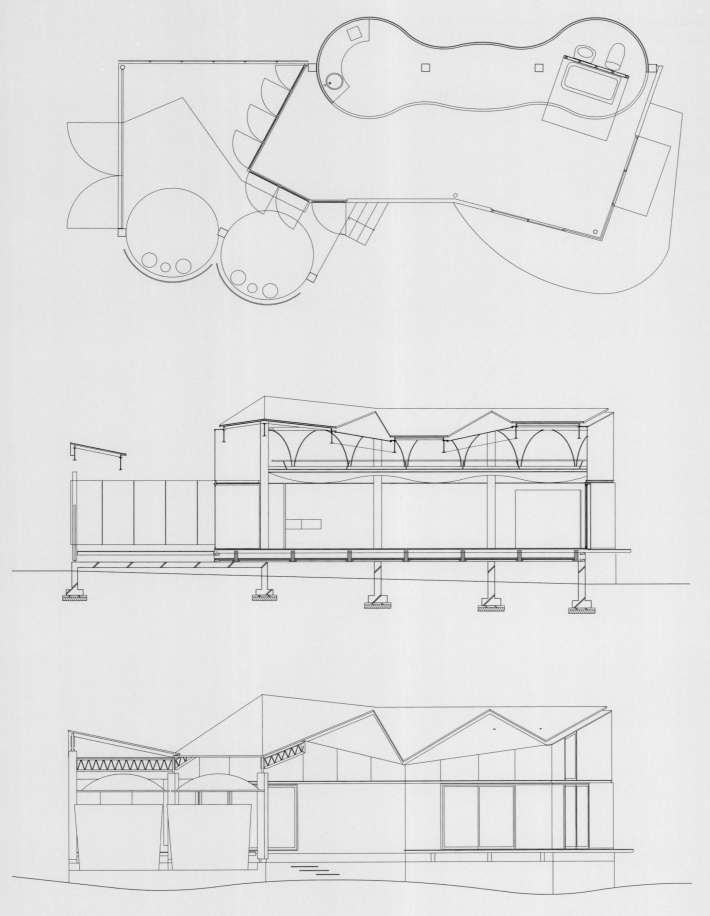

Saishunkan Seiyaku Women's Dormitory
Kumamoto, Japan 1990–91

This dormitory for eighty employees of a company in western Japan is reserved exclusively for women in their first year with the firm. This training period is meant to foster a team spirit and the objective is reflected in the architectural forms adopted. The only private spaces are the bedrooms, each of which sleeps four, while the core of the building is a large common room. All the smaller rooms are directly linked to this main area. The toilets, a collective bathroom, and the utilities are inserted as separate volumes jutting into the large central room. In this way they form a series of spaces that break up the common room and encourage the residents to extend their personal spheres into its different niches. Women living in the building experience the whole range of subtle variations between public and private spaces.

Detail of the north front and nighttime view from the northwest.

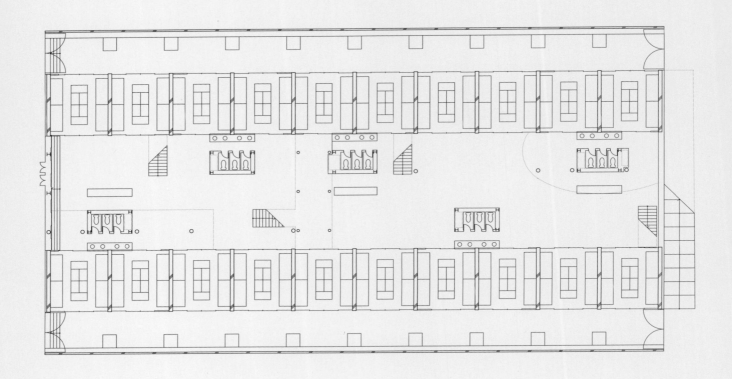

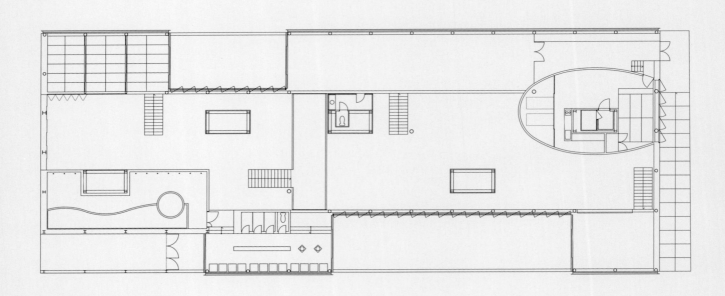

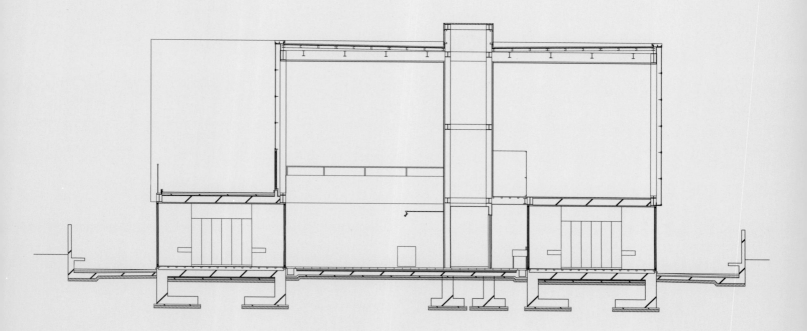

Plans of the first and second
floors, and cross section.

View of the large common-room
with open toilets, and detail
of the air ducts.

View and reverse angle
of the central hall with
the kitchen-dining area and
the catwalk to the terrace outside.

Gifu Kitagata Apartment Building
Gifu, Japan 1994–2000

This public housing block is located in Gifu prefecture and forms part of a complex designed by Arata Isozaki. Coordinating the project, Isozaki chose four women architects and commissioned a building from each.

The fundamental concept behind the master plan was to arrange the apartment buildings along the perimeter of the area so as to enclose a space for collective use. For this reason the architects sought to pare the building down to the narrowest possible volume. At the same time, the brief called for a large floor surface and also a building with a compact cross section, which would have made it appear rather massive. It was decided to get around this difficulty by creating voids in the building and visually linking the front with the rear to heighten the impression of its slender proportions.

A fairly simple system made it possible to insert home units of different sizes. Each apartment is the sum of smaller units combined. The basic cell is a studio apartment defined by the structure of the building. Antechambers on the south façade link a number of cells to form the different apartments, while external galleries running along the north elevation provide access to the home units. Not only the individual apartments but even each room is potentially accessible from a door opening onto the gallery, making the homes flexible and capable of providing for the most disparate kinds of family groups. The layouts and dimensions of the units are masked on the north façade along the street-front, but clearly identifiable on the internal elevation looking south.

Detail of the galleries and view from the south.

Detail of the terraces running through the building.

View of the north front with stairs and galleries.

174

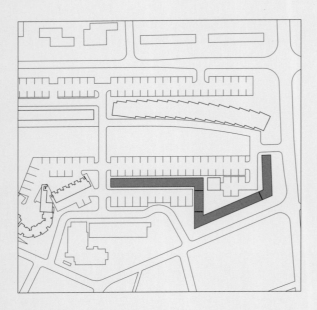

General layout and plan
of the standard floor.

Elevations of the housing complex.

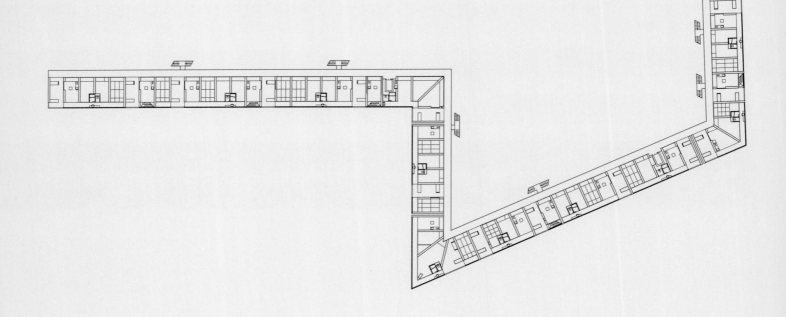

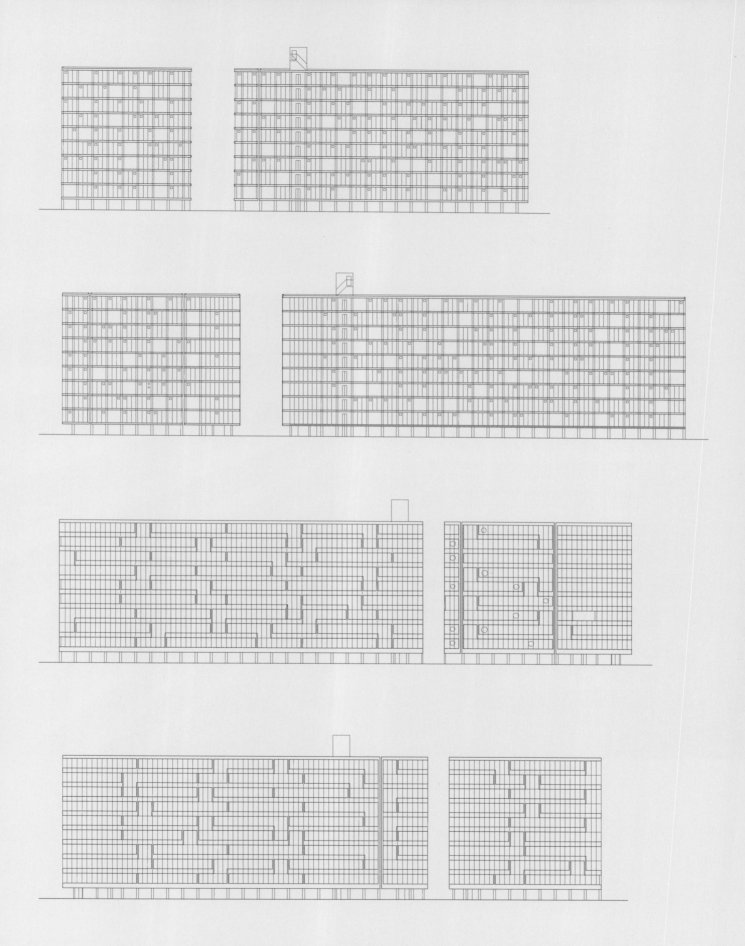

Detail of the passages that distribute the interiors of the units on the main front.

Diagrammatic developments
of the longitudinal sections along
the floors on the north and south
fronts, and along the central axis
of the housing block.

Detail of the longitudinal section.

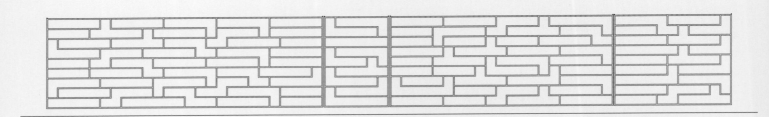

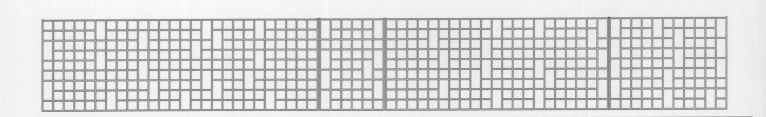

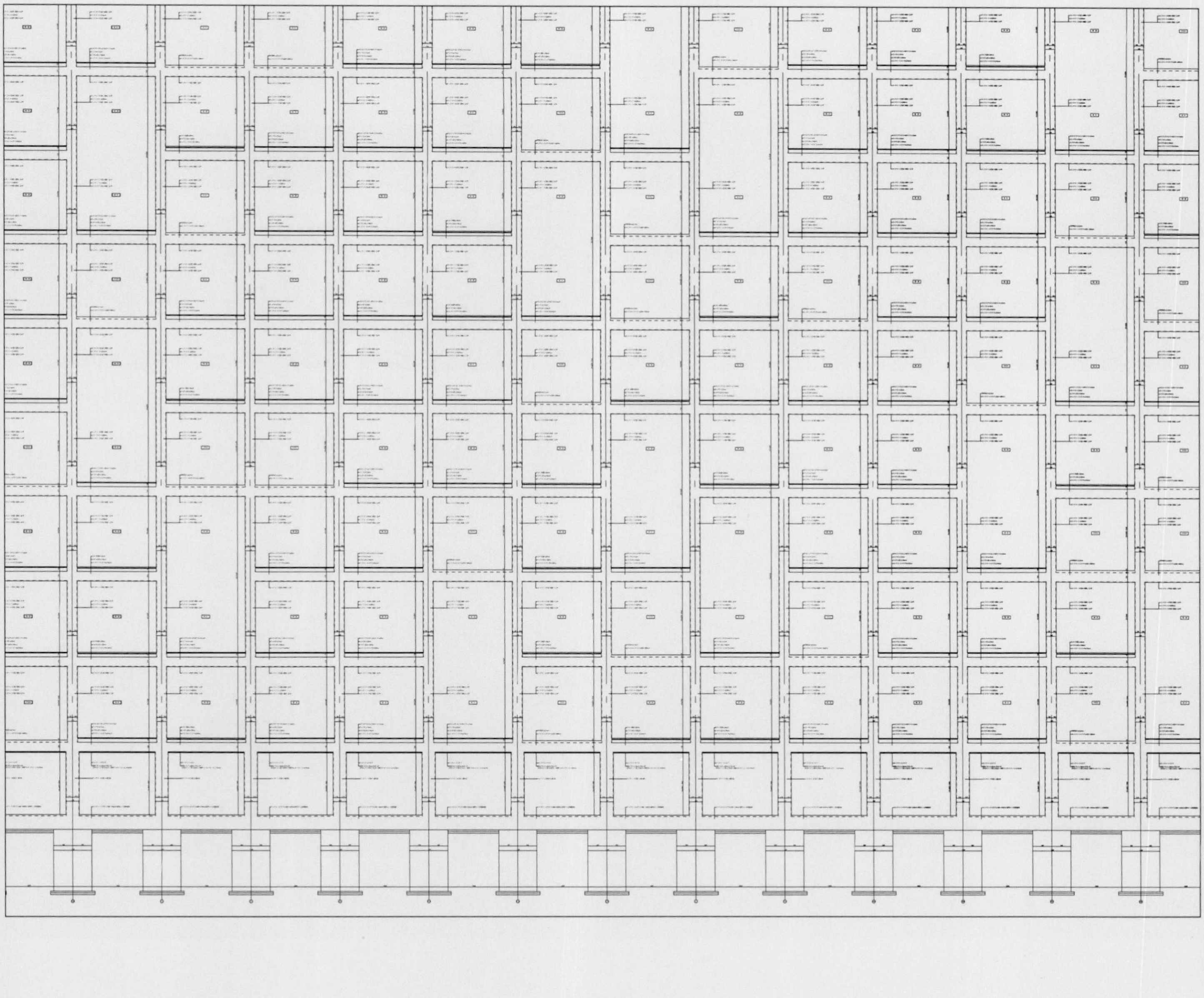

Passage in a unit
on the south front.

The interior of a duplex flat
and view of a linking terrace.

Small House
Tokyo, Japan 1999–2000

This small house is in one of Tokyo's most up-market districts. Since the lot is extremely small and expensive it was decided to tailor the house to the needs of the clients. The family that ordered the project were clear about the functions they wanted, with the house divided into four rooms superimposed to create four different levels.

In structural terms, the staircase set in the middle of the building is the principal load-bearing member.

It unobtrusively determines the layouts of the various floors. Beginning with the basement level and rising to the top, the list of rooms comprises the master bedroom, a supplementary room for the future children, a family/kitchen/dining room, and a terrace with the laundry. Each floor and its relationship with the central staircase are specifically designed to match its corresponding function. These design decisions were then refined to provide

for other needs: the link between interior and exterior, the car park and a small courtyard on the semi-basement level. Viewed from outside, the distinctive form of the building is largely determined by the positioning of the windows and the zigzagging of the infill panels, which join floor and ceilings skewed off axis. In such small interiors, variations of just a few centimeters make a big difference to their functionality.

Aerial view and view from the northwest.

Daytime and nighttime views
of the east front.

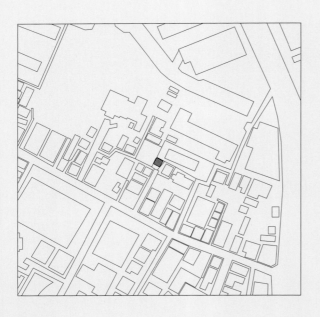

General layout and plans
of the first and second floors,
basement level and third floor.

South, north, west, east fronts,
and eastwest and northsouth
sections.

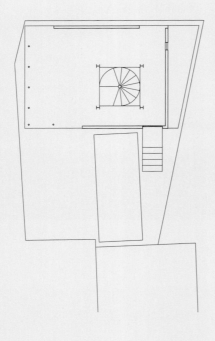

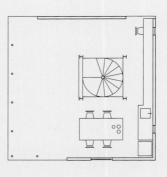

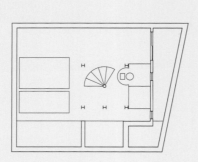

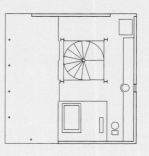

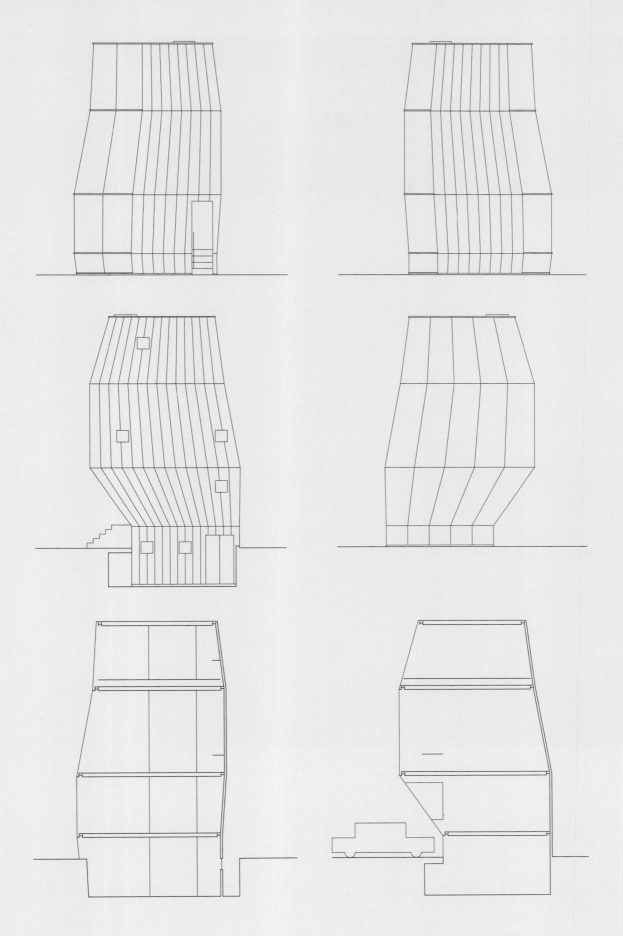

189

Details of the fronts and
view of the bathroom
and of the covered roof terrace.

House Surrounded by Plum Trees
Tokyo, Japan 2001–03

This small house was planned for a young couple with two children and their grandmother. The lot is located in a peaceful residential district on the outskirts of Tokyo. The clients wanted a home that would look like a single connected space. They also wanted a building that protected the existing setting, so they could enjoy a view of the plum trees growing on the site. To meet these needs the volume of the building was reduced to a minimum and set in the middle of the plot with the trees ranged around its edges. In most private homes there is usually a conventional fixed ratio between the number of occupants and the number of rooms. Here, instead of grouping the various functions in specialized zones, each function was set in a different room. The spaces, strictly defined in geometrical and functional terms, are also connected by being partially opening onto each other. This creates an intermediate layout between the series of small rooms and the open-plan space.

The walls between the rooms are structural sheets of steel just 16 millimeters thick. The outer walls employ the same steel sheets with the addition of an insulating layer and are faced with chalkboard for an overall thickness of 50 millimeters. The space cells were prefabricated and simply assembled in situ. Thin walls were an essential part of the project for practical reasons as well as being a way to reduce its visual mass. They admit multiple apertures and are unobtrusive. The layout of the spaces and positions of the openings leave the occupants great freedom to create new links between the rooms and their interrelated functions. This enables them to experience a unique combination of togetherness and privacy.

North and south fronts.

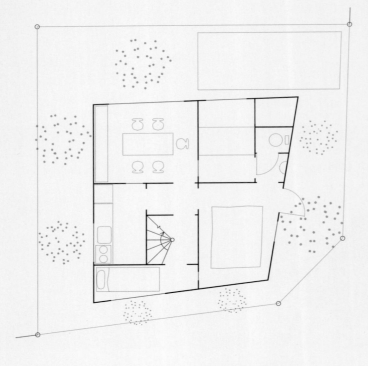

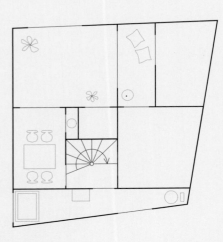

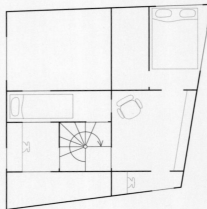

General layout and plans
of the first, second, and
third floors.

Sections and fronts:
northeast, northwest, southeast,
and southwest.

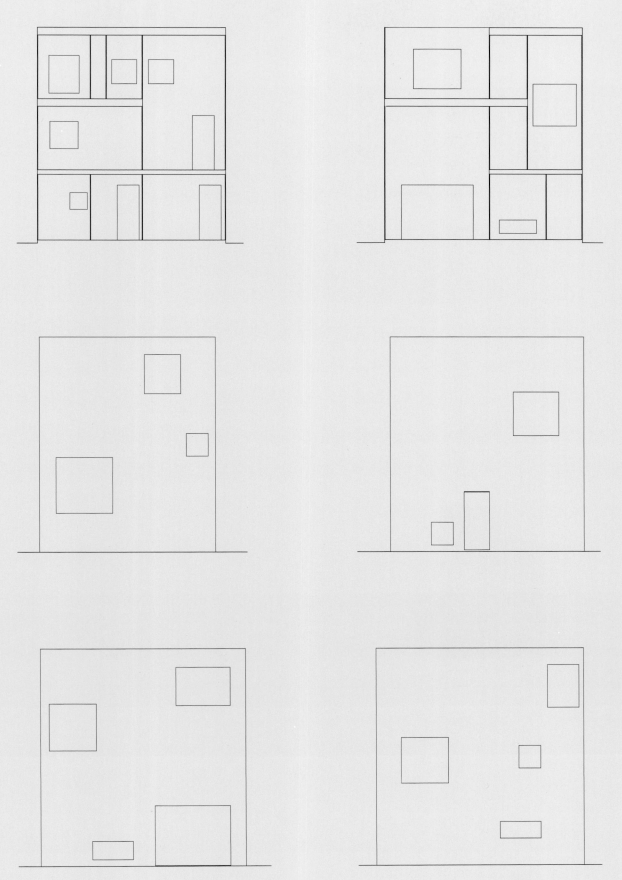

Views of the library,
of the meditation room,
and of the roof terrace.

View of the terrace.

Onishi Civic Center

Gunma, Japan, 2003–05

The project consists in a public multi-functional facility for the city of Onishi, in Gunma province, three hours by train from Tokyo. The complex includes a gymnasium, auditorium, and offices. These functions are laid out in three curvilinear glass volumes, each with a highly articulated form that makes it difficult to grasp its real dimensions. The blocks are clustered together and interlock with to define internal and external spaces of different shapes and sizes. Though they grouped and managed as a single facility, the buildings are functionally independent. The site lies above a large grassy area in the heart of this small town and the design sought to protect the impression of an open, unbroken space, despite the presence of this large complex. To achieve this, the biggest facilities, such as the gymnasium and the auditorium, were set partially below ground level. This enabled the building's overall height to be kept low, in harmony with the horizontal lines of the setting.

Visitors skirting the area can observe the activities going on inside the buildings. The image of nature filtered through the space below the floating roofs links the interiors to the park outside.

General view of the model and view from the south.

Detail of the south front and view from northeast.

Gym pavilion.

External and internal views
of the foyer of the auditorium.

Detail of the walkways between
the pavilions and interior of the
gym on the semi-basement level.

Detail of the façades.

Office of Ryue Nishizawa

Weekend House
Gunma, Japan 1997–98

This weekend house stands in an area of peaceful woodland. Its dark, squared profile appears immersed in the surrounding forest land. The house is placed almost in the middle of a large glade, but for safety reasons it was decided to limit the number of doors and windows. Because of this three patios of different sizes were added. The plan of the building is based on a structural grid 2.40 meters square and it is divided into rooms separated by the three courts, which bring light into them. The walls and ceilings are made respectively of glass and a plastic material: this diffuses the shimmer of the greenery from the gardens through the house, evoking its natural surroundings. The reflection of the vegetation follows you as you move through the house and the movement also seems to subtly transform the spaces.

View from northeast and part of the west front.

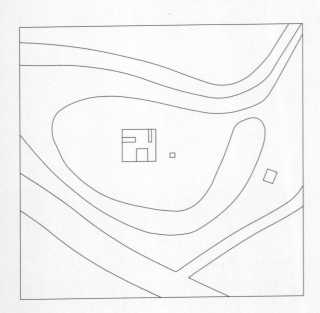

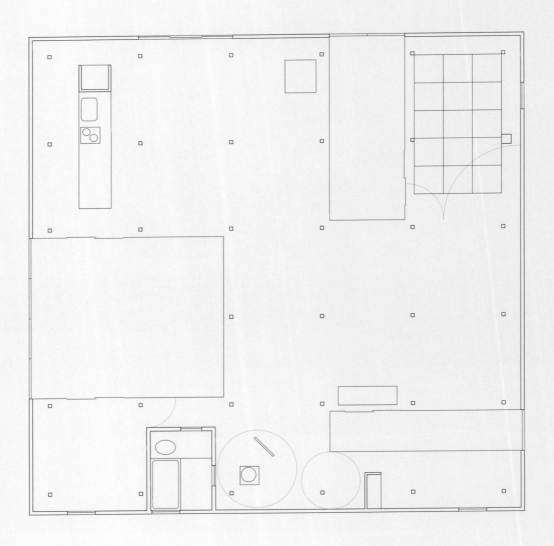

General layout and plan.

Cross section and longitudinal section on the north patio.

Views of the interiors.

House at Kamakura

Kanagawa, Japan 1999–2001

This house is located in a suburb of Tokyo, in an area immersed in greenery. The building occupies one of the lots of a line of residences in a valley bottom covered with large trees, between the forest in front and a steep slope behind it.

The building is laid out on two semi-basement levels. The lower level contains a living room and study, while the bedroom is on the upper level. A cellar provides extra storage space. The neighboring houses are set at a slight angle to the road. The plan of the house was deformed into a parallelogram to keep the same distance on either side and have its principal elevations face onto the road and forest. Its form is shaped by features in its immediate context. On the inside, the trapezoidal plan creates a narrowing or enlarged vista, depending on which way you look.

The rooms are painted light green, using a slightly phosphorescent paint. The walls absorb and register variations in the light and in the evening, when darkness falls, for some minutes they reflect traces of the movements within the house.

Views of the southeast front.

Daytime and nighttime views
of the living room from the street.

View of the first-floor living room.

General layout and plans
of the first and second floors.

Longitudinal section and fronts:
northeast and southeast.

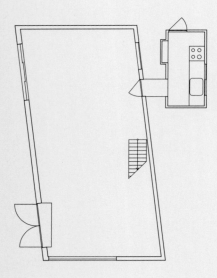

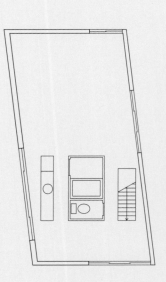

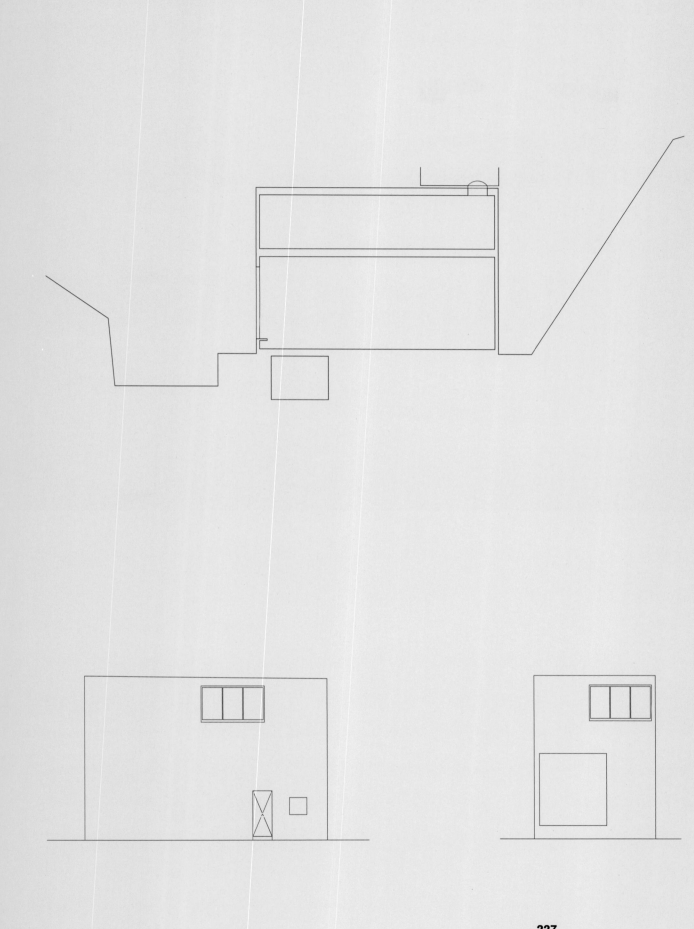

Roof access from the
bedroom and the glow
of the phosphorescent plaster
at sunset.

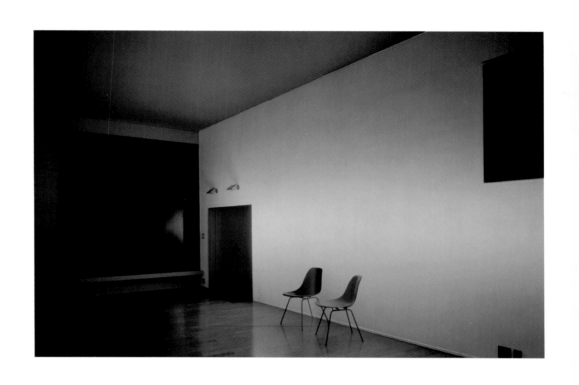

Moriyama House

Tokyo, Japan 2002–present

The Moriyama House consists of the client's private home, as well as a cluster of five rental homes. The scale of the district in which they are set is defined by two- or three-story buildings, low-rise apartment blocks and one-family homes, neatly aligned and alternating with small voids. They are quality lots, which create a typically Japanese urban atmosphere.

If the brief had called for the construction a single volume on the site, it would have looked out of scale with the surrounding urban fabric. So it was decided to build separate and independent units. This related the development to the morphology of the context, with the serried reiteration of closed buildings and narrow passages between them. This solution allowed each unit to have a small garden.

The layouts of the different buildings and the form and size of the rooms vary freely. The units planned include: one development on three levels; another one on a square plan, set partially underground; one with very high ceilings; one entirely surrounded by gardens; and various kinds of home units. The blocks are set close to each other, but with interstices between them, like alleys or even wider, for the gardens. In this way, each cell establishes relations with its setting. It was decided not to create spaces that were not closed on themselves but capable of creating a flow between interior and garden or alley, in a way traditionally characteristic of housing in Tokyo.

The model from above.

The model from southeast and study sketches.

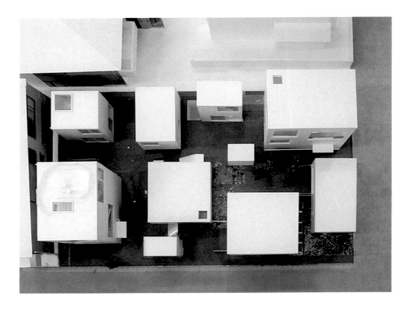

The open interstitial areas
between the home units.

Plan laid out on the building
lot and views of construction.

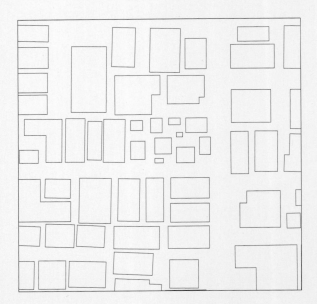

General plan, cross section
of the bathroom, of the party room
and living room, and view
from northeast.

Plans of first and second floors.

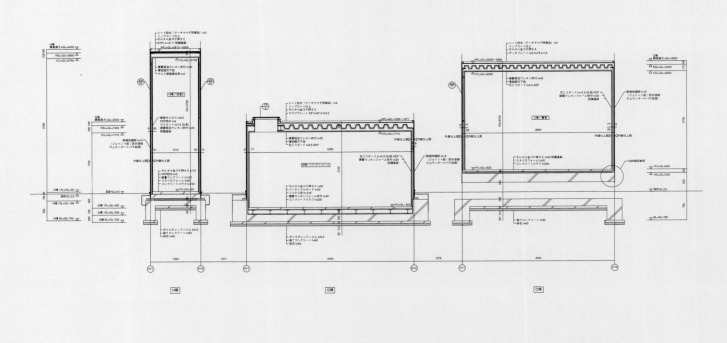

H棟   G棟／パーティルーム   C棟／居間室

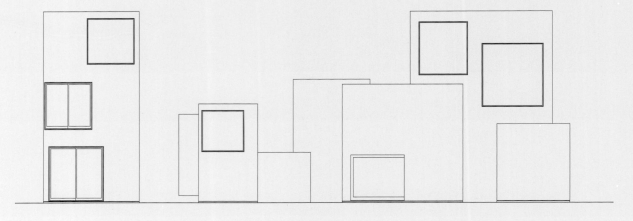

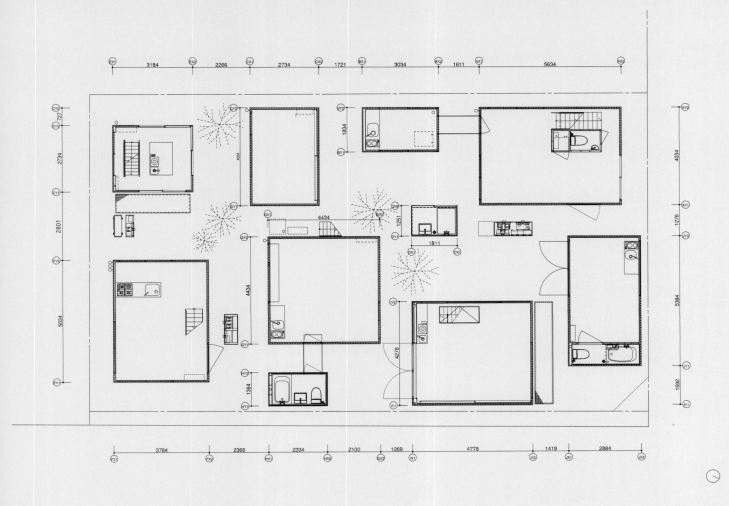

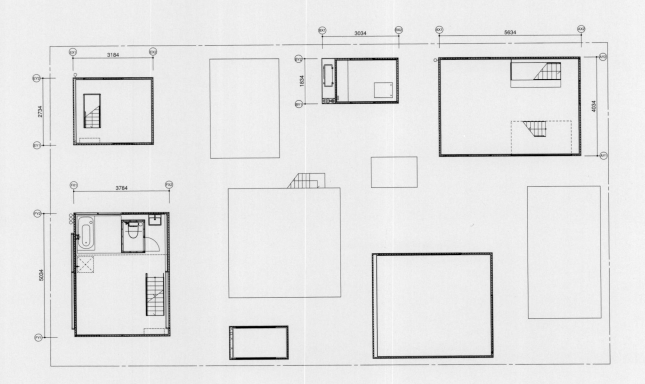

A-House
Tokyo, Japan 2004–present

This house is situated in the Tokyo metropolitan area. The lot is long and narrow, running north to south. On the right and left, the adjacent residences stand a short distance away. The client wanted a living room for guests, a second living room large enough to hold private parties, bedrooms, a bathroom, kitchen, and storeroom. The first step was to decide the forms and dimensions of the various rooms on the basis of factors such as their use and furnishings.

The five rooms of different sizes were arranged in a logical sequence, slightly staggered so as to secure natural lighting and ventilation for the whole building. In this house, each room is conceived as a living space: one is large and open, another closed and intimate; there is a spacious bathroom and a kitchen/dining-room opening onto a garden. The object was create a comfortable and relaxing series of domestic spaces.

Longitudinal section and sequence of the plans of the different rooms.

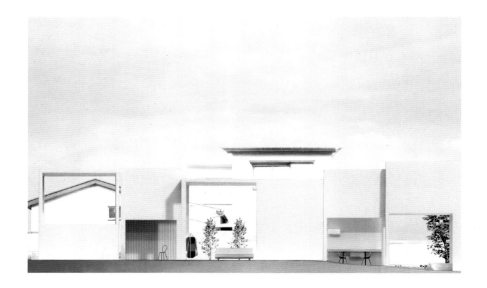

View of the vertical section
of the model.

Plans of the first and second
floors, longitudinal section
and lateral elevation.

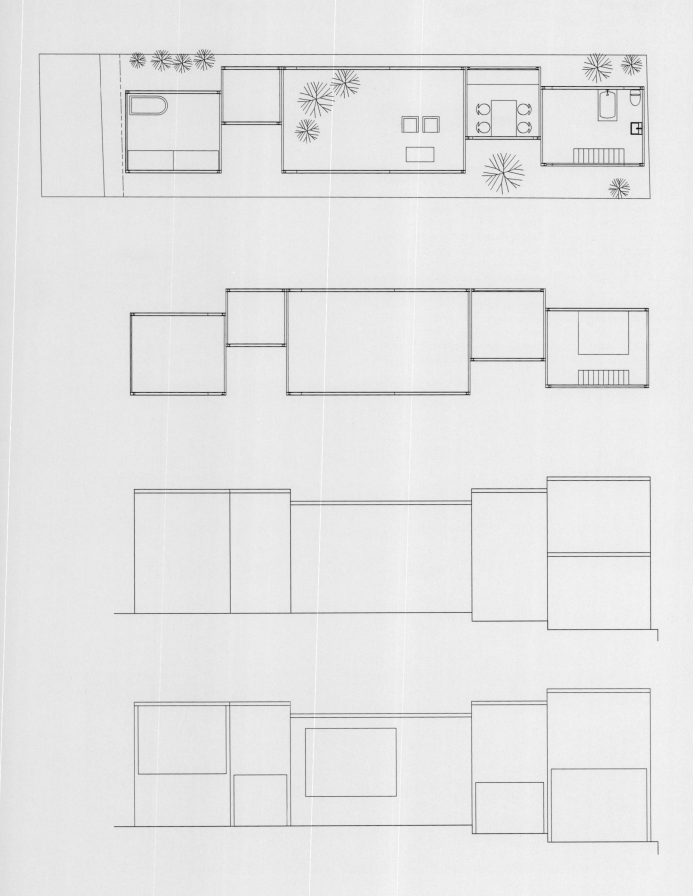

Naoshima Museum
Kagawa, Japan 2005–present

This private museum of contemporary art stands on the island of Naoshima, in the Sea of Japan. Unlike most museums, the building consists of a single large room containing two permanent collections. The subject of one of the collections is sound, of the other color. The client wanted an architecture capable of integrating the works of art in a single space based on light. To do this, without disturbing the aura of the exhibits, it was decided to create a chamber of indefinite size, entirely immersed in light, using a concrete shell 20 centimeters thick. Inside, the form of this extraordinary room, completely devoid of corners, is indecipherable at first sight.

The museum is not a work of art in itself, but a background. At the same time the intention was not just to create a setting but to evoke a special dimension, a space of unbounded vastness, like the boundless universe. An architecture so conceived should communicate nothing, ultimately, other than the presence of art and light.

Building site and the interior of the exhibition room.

Glimpse of the roof between
the landforms and photomontage
of the digital model on the site.

View of the "teardrop"
model-concept and general plan.

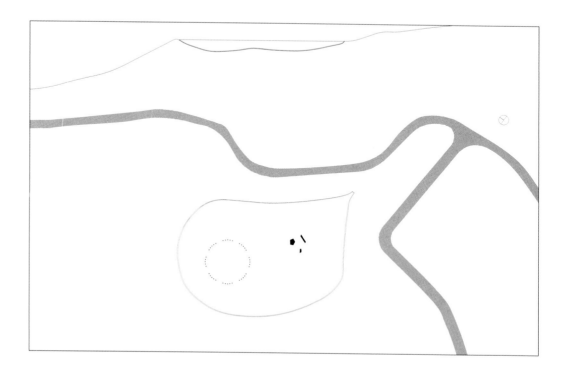

appendices

list of works

SANAA [Kazuyo Sejima + Ryue Nishizawa]

Multimedia Studio, Gifu, Japan 1995–96
surface area of site: 22,347 sqm
built surface area: 856 sqm
indoor surface area: 873 sqm

N Museum, Wakayama, Japan 1995–97
with Jin Hosoya, Yoshitaka Tanase
engineers: Matsui Gengo + O.R.S. Office (structural),
ES Associates (mechanical);
Nichiei Projects (electrical)
surface area of site: 4,000 sqm
built surface area: 752 sqm
indoor surface area: 752 sqm

O Museum, Nagano, Japan 1995–99
with Yoshitaka Tanase
engineers: Sasaki Structural Consultants / Mutsuro Sasaki,
Shuji Tada (structural); ES Associates (mechanical);
Nichiei Projects (electrical)
surface area of site: 4,487 sqm
built surface area: 435 sqm
indoor surface area: 458 sqm

S House, Okayama, Japan 1995–96
surface area of site: 131 sqm
built surface area: 87 sqm
indoor surface area: 142 sqm

Park Café, Ibaraki, Japan 1997–98
with Yoshitaka Tanase, Go Kuwata
engineers: Sasaki Structural Consultants / Mutsuro Sasaki,
Yasutaka Konishi (structural); System Design Laboratory
(mechanical); Nichiei Projects (electrical)
surface area of site: 210,000 sqm
built surface area: 262 sqm
indoor surface area: 262 sqm

M House, Tokyo, Japan 1996–97
surface area of site: 207 sqm
built surface area: 112 sqm
indoor surface area: 215 sqm

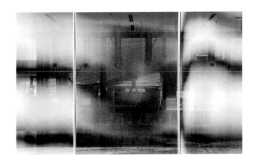

Welfare Center, Kanagawa, Japan 1997
surface area of site: 3,062 sqm
built surface area: 900 sqm
indoor surface area: 994 sqm

K Office Building, Ibaraki, Japan 1996–97
surface area of site: 687 sqm
built surface area: 473 sqm
indoor surface area: 2,817 sqm

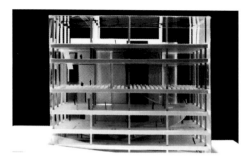

**Project for the Museum of Contemporary Art,
Sydney, Australia 1997–99**
surface area of site: 1,482 sqm
built surface area: 1,089 sqm
indoor surface area: 8,756 sqm

**Project for the New Campus Center
of the Illinois Institute of Technology,
Chicago, Illinois, United States 1998**
surface area of site: 20,300 sqm
built surface area: 10,665 sqm
indoor surface area: 10,665 sqm

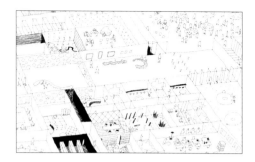

**De Kunstlinie Theater and Cultural Center,
Almere, Holland 1998–present**
with Yoshitaka Tanase (director), Go Kuwata,
Jonas Elding, Yoritaka Hayashi, Hiroshi Kikuchi,
Florian Idenburg, Fenna Haakma Wagnaar
engineers: Adviesbureau voor Bouwtechniek bv;
Sasaki Structural Consultants / Mutsuro Sasaki,
Masahiro Ikeda, Hiroki Kume, Shuji Tada,
Yasutaka Konishi, ABT Consulting Engineers v.o.f (structural);
Technical management BV (mechanical);
DHV Consultant (acoustics); Janssen and Motosugi Theater
consultants v.o.f (stage engineering); v2bo (fire protection)
surface area of site: 15,354 sqm
built surface area: 9,261 sqm
indoor surface area: 19,085 sqm

**Proposal for Reclaiming Salerno's Inner City,
Italy 1999–present**
competition, ranked first
built surface area: 2,788 sqm
indoor surface area: 2,788 sqm

21st Century Museum of Contemporary Art, Kanazawa, Ishikawa, Japan 1999–2004
with Toshihiro Yoshimura, Yoshifumi Kojima,
Koichiro Tokimori, Kansuke Kawashima, Tetsuo Kondo,
Shoko Fukuya, Mizuki Imamura, Naoki Hori, Junya Ishigami,
Erika Hidaka, Keizo Eki
engineers: Sasaki Structural Consultants / Mutsuro Sasaki,
Yasutaka Konishi (structural); ES Associates (mechanical);
P.T. Morimura & Associates, LTD (electrical);
Central Consultant Inc. (car parking)
surface area of site: 26,010 sqm
built surface area: 9,616 sqm
indoor surface area: 17,364 sqm

Prada Beauty Store, Arezzo, Italy 2000
built surface area: 30 sqm
indoor surface area: 30 sqm

**Installation of the Japan Pavilion
at the Venice Biennale, Italy 2000**

Lumiere Park Café, Almere, Holland 1999–present
surface area of site: 10,611 sqm
built surface area: 377 sqm
indoor surface area: 376.58 sqm

Dior Omotesando Store, Tokyo, Japan 2001–03
with Junya Ishigami, Koichiro Tokimori, Yumiko Yamada,
Yoshitaka Tanase, Erika Hidaka
engineers: Sasaki Structural Consultants / Mutsuro Sasaki,
Hiroki Kume, Shuji Tada, Ayumi Isozaki (structural);
P.T. Morimura & Associates, LTD (mechanical);
KILT Planning Group (illuminated signs);
Christian Dior Couture Architectural,
Department Architecture & Associé, H&A (interior design)
surface area of site: 315 sqm
built surface area: 274 sqm
indoor surface area: 1,492 sqm

**Glass Pavilion at the Toledo Museum of Art,
Toledo, Ohio, United States 2001–present**
with Florian Idenbrug, Toshihiro Oki, Junya Ishigami,
Keiko Uchiyama, Takayuki Hasegawa, Yutaka Kikuchi,
Tetsuo Kondo
engineers: Kendall/Heaton Associates, Inc.;
Paratus Group (administration);
SAPS – Sasaki and Partners / Mutsuro Sasaki, Masahiro Ikeda,
Eisuke Mitsuda, Guy Nordenson and Associates (structural);
Consentini Associates (mechanical);
The Mannik & Smith Group, Inc. (civil engineering);
Front Inc. (façade systems), KILT Planning Group, ARUP lighting
(lighting); Harvey Marshall Associates (acoustics); Layne
Consultants (engineers);
Inside Outside (screening systems)
surface area of site: 19,300 sqm
built surface area: 3,257 sqm
indoor surface area: 6,832 sqm

**Project for the Extension to the Rietberg Museum,
Zurich, Switzerland 2002**
competition, ranked first
surface area of site: 12,242 sqm
built surface area: 2,625 sqm
indoor surface area: 3,144 sqm

**Extension to the Instituto Valenciano de Arte Moderno,
Valencia, Spain 2002–present**
with Yoshitaka Tanase (director), Yumiko Yamada,
Rikiya Yamamoto, Hiroaki Katagiri
engineers: Área Ingeniería y Arquitectura S.L.;
SAPS – Sasaki and Partners / Mutsuro Sasaki,
Masahiro Ikeda, Yasutaka Konishi, Hirofumi Ohno,
Mitsutaka Inagaki (structural consultants); Obio,
Moya y Asociados, S.L. (structural); IDOM (mechanical);
GBBM (acoustics); ARUP (environmental consultants);
ARUP Lighting (lighting)
surface area of site: 8,522 sqm
built surface area: 8,105 sqm
indoor surface area: 42,646 sqm

**Project for the New Mercedes-Benz Museum,
Stuttgart, Germany 2002**
competition, ranked second
surface area of site: 62,000 sqm
built surface area: 15,752 sqm
indoor surface area: 25,140 sqm

Issey Miyake Store by Naoki Takizawa, Tokyo, Japan 2003
built surface area: 118 sqm
indoor surface area: 118 sqm

Naoshima Ferry Terminal, Kagawa, Japan 2003–present
with Rikiya Yamamoto
engineers: Sasaki Structural Consutants / Mutsuro Sasaki, Ayumi Isozaki, Eisuke Mitsuda (structural);
Kankyo Engineering (mechanical)
surface area of site: 5,364 sqm
built surface area: 3,671 sqm
indoor surface area: 1,939 sqm

Zollverein School of Design, Essen, Germany 2003–present
with Yoshitaka Tanase (director), Nicole Berganski, Osamu Kato, Andreas Krawczyk, Jonas Elding, Karen Schütz, Junya Ishigami, Hiroaki Katagiri
engineers: Dipl.-Ing. BöllArchitekt;
SAPS – Sasaki and Partners / Mutsuro Sasaki, Hiroki Kume, Masahiro Ikeda (structural consultants);
Bollinger + Grohmann (structural); Transplan / Transsolar (mechanical); Horstmann + Berger (environmental consultants);
Müller-BBM (acoustics)
surface area of site: 14,694 sqm
built surface area: 1,433 sqm
indoor surface area: 7,098 sqm

New Museum of Contemporary Art New York, United States, 2003–present
with Florian Idenburg, Jonas Elding, Javier Haddad Conde, Koji Yoshida, Hiroaki Katagiri, Toshihiro Oki, Kansuke Kawashima, Andreas Krawczyk, Junya Ishigami, Yoritaka Hayashi, Yoshitaka Tanase, Fenna Haakma Wagenaar, Jamin Morrison
engineers: Guggenheimer Projects (SD1);
SAPS – Sasaki and Partners / Mutsuro Sasaki, Eisuke Mitsuda, Hajime Narukawa (structural consultants);
Guy Nordenson and Associates (structural); ARUP (mechanical);
Tillotson Design Associates (lighting);
Front Inc. (façade systems)
surface area of site: 738 sqm
built surface area: 738 sqm
indoor surface area: 5,776 sqm

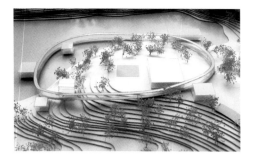

Novartis Office Building, Basel, Switzerland 2003–present
competition, ranked second
with Yoshitaka Tanase (director), Nicole Berganski, Takayuki
Hasegawa, Yuka Nishiyama, Isao Shinohara, Koji Yoshida
engineers: Arcoplan; SAPS – Sasaki and Partners / Mutsuro
Sasaki, Yasutaka Konishi, Takeshi Suzuki, Bollinger + Grohmann
(structural); Transplan / Transsolar (mechanical); Horstmann +
Berger (acoustics); Front Inc., Neuschwander + Morf
(façade systems)
surface area of site: 1,059 sqm
built surface area: 1,059 sqm
indoor surface area: 7,907 sqm

**Learning Center of the École Polytechnique Fédérale
de Lausanne, Lausanne, Switzerland 2005–present**
with Tetsuo Kondo, Yumiko Yamada, Koichiro Tokimori,
Rikiya Yamamoto, Osamu Kato, Mizuko Kaji,
Yoshitaka Tanase, Yuki Tamura, Takashi Suo, Julien Broussart
engineers: Proplanning; SAPS – Sasaki and Partners / Mutsuro
Sasaki, Ayumi Isozaki, Eisuke Mitsuda (structural consultants);
B&G (structural)
surface area of site: 83,300 sqm
built surface area: 15,900 sqm
indoor surface area: 39,000 sqm

**House for the CIPEA (China International Practical
Exhibition of Architecture),
Nanjing, China 2004–present**
surface area of site: 4,224 sqm
built surface area: 747 sqm
indoor surface area: 818 sqm

Kazuyo Sejima & Associates

**Platform I Vacation House,
Chiba, Japan 1987–88**
surface area of site: 541 sqm
built surface area: 108 sqm
indoor surface area: 120 sqm

Platform II Studio, Yamanashi, Japan 1988–90
with Ako Nagao
engineers: T.I.S. & Partners (structural)
surface area of site: 661 sqm
built surface area: 47 sqm
indoor surface area: 67 sqm

**Project for Platform III House,
Tokyo, Japan 1989–90**
surface area of site: 192 sqm
built surface area: 105 sqm
indoor surface area: 312 sqm

**Castelbajac Sports Store,
Kanagawa, Japan 1990–91**
surface area of site: 97 sqm
built surface area: 71 sqm
indoor surface area: 100,38 sqm

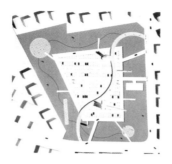

**Standard Project for an Apartment Building,
Osaka, Japan 1991**
built surface area: 91 sqm
indoor surface area: 84 sqm

**Saishunkan Seiyaku Women's Dormitory,
Kumamoto, Japan 1990–91**
with Ryue Nishizawa
engineers: Matsui Gengo + O.R.S. Office (structural);
System Design Laboratory (mechanical)
surface area of site: 1,223 sqm
built surface area: 852 sqm
indoor surface area: 1,257 sqm

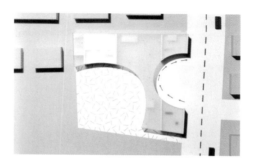

**Project for the Nasunogahara Harmony Hall,
Tochigi, Japan 1991**
competition
surface area of site: 25,037 sqm
built surface area: 6300 sqm
indoor surface area: 8490 sqm

N House, Kumamoto, Japan 1990–92
surface area of site: 1,053 sqm
built surface area: 435 sqm
indoor surface area: 639 sqm

Pachinko Parlor I, Ibaraki, Japan 1991–93
surface area of site: 598 sqm
built surface area: 517 sqm
indoor surface area: 993 sqm

Y House, Chiba, Japan 1993–94
surface area of site: 172 sqm
built surface area: 70 sqm
indoor surface area: 152 sqm

Villa in the Forest, Nagano, Japan 1992–94
surface area of site: 1,260 sqm
built surface area: 156 sqm
indoor surface area: 199 sqm

**Police Office in Chofu Station,
Tokyo, Japan 1993–94**
surface area of site: 71 sqm
built surface area: 40 sqm
indoor surface area: 56 sqm

**Pachinko Parlor II,
Ibaraki, Japan 1993**
surface area of site: 3784 sqm
built surface area: 165 sqm
indoor surface area: 165 sqm

**Project for a Service Center at the Tokyo Expo 96,
Tokyo, Japan 1994–95**
surface area of site: 141,512 sqm
built surface area: 7,254 sqm
indoor surface area: 7,300 sqm

**Gifu Kitagata Apartment Building,
Gifu, Japan 1994–2000**
with Koichiro Tokimori, Yoshifumi Kojima
engineers: O.R.S. Office (structural);
Asano Setsubi (mechanical)
surface area of site: 34,647 sqm
built surface area: (I) 585 sqm, (II) 592 sqm
indoor surface area: (I) 4,706 sqm, (II) 4,755 sqm

Studies for Metropolitan Housing, 1994–95

**Pachinko Parlor III,
Ibaraki, Japan 1995–96**
surface area of site: 4,042 sqm
built surface area: 681 sqm
indoor surface area: 794 sqm

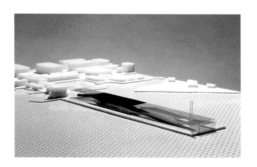

**Project for the International Terminal
of Yokohama Port, Kanagawa, Japan 1994**
competition, ranked third
surface area of site: 33,040 sqm
indoor surface area: 48,000 sqm

U Office Building, Ibaraki, Japan 1996–98
surface area of site: 1,172 sqm
built surface area: 506 sqm
indoor surface area: 2,750 sqm

**Kozankaku Student Residence,
Ibaraki, Japan 1999–2000**
surface area of site: 72,797 sqm
built surface area: 263 sqm
indoor surface area: 263 sqm

Small House, Tokyo, Japan 1999–2000
with Yoshitaka Tanase, Shoko Fukuya
engineers: Sasaki Structural Consultants / Mutsuro Sasaki,
Shuji Tada, Eisuke Mitsuda (structural)
surface area of site: 60 sqm
built surface area: 34 sqm
indoor surface area: 77 sqm

**hhstyle.com Store,
Tokyo, Japan 1999–2000**
surface area of site: 378 sqm
built surface area: 263 sqm
indoor surface area: 830 sqm

**Asahi Shimbun Yamagata Office Building,
Yamagata, Japan 2000–02**
surface area of site: 572 sqm
built surface area: 227 sqm
indoor surface area: 708 sqm

Onishi Civic Center, Gunma, Japan, 2003–05
with Koichiro Tokimori, Yutaka Kikuchi, Rikiya Yamamoto,
Tetsuo Kondo, Junya Ishigami
engineers: Kawaguchi & Engineers (structural);
System Design Laboratory, Uichi Inoue Mechanical Consultants,
Setsubi Keikaku Mechanical Consultants (mechanical)
surface area of site: 8,850 sqm
built surface area: 2,020 sqm
indoor surface area: 2,276 sqm

**House Surrounded by Plum Trees
Tokyo, Japan 2001–03**
with Yoshitaka Tanase, Koji Yoshida,
Junya Ishigami, Taeko Nakatsubo
engineers: Sasaki Structural Consultants / Mutsuro Sasaki,
Yasutaka Konishi, Takeshi Suzuki (structural);
System Design Laboratory (mechanical)
surface area of site: 92 sqm
built surface area: 37 sqm
indoor surface area: 78 sqm

Office of Ryue Nishizawa

Weekend House,
Gunma, Japan 1997–98
with Kimihiko Okada
engineers: Structured Environment-Alan Burden (structural);
System Design Laboratory-Akiko Sano (mechanical)
built surface area: 130 sqm
indoor surface area: 130 sqm

Takeo Head Office Store,
Tokyo, Japan 1999–2000
indoor surface area: 608 sqm

House at Kamakura, Kanagawa,
Japan 1999–2001
with Kimihiko Okada
engineers: Structured Environment-Alan Burden,
Noriko Tsutagawa (structural);
System Design Laboratory-Akiko Sano (mechanical)
surface area of site: 140 sqm
built surface area: 50 sqm
indoor surface area: 103 sqm

**Apartment Building at Ichikawa,
Chiba, Japan 2001–present**
surface area of site: 327 sqm
built surface area:100 sqm
indoor surface area: 268 sqm

Moriyama House, Tokyo, Japan 2002–present
with Ippei Takahashi, Kimihiko Okada, Yusuke Ohi
engineers: Structured Environment / Alan Burden,
Hirohide Tao, Taizen Nieda (structural);
Kankyo Engineering / Masakazu Gokita,
Tsugihisa Narita (mechanical)
surface area of site: 290 sqm
built surface area: 130 sqm
indoor surface area: 263 sqm

**Eda Apartment Building, Kanagawa,
Japan 2002–present**
surface area of site: 3,195 sqm
built surface area: 2,162 sqm
indoor surface area: 8,860 sqm

Love Planet Museum, Okayama, Japan 2003
indoor surface area: 129 sqm

**Funabashi Apartment Building,
Chiba, Japan 2002–04**
surface area of site: 340 sqm
built surface area: 243 sqm
indoor surface area: 649 sqm

Video Pavilion, Kagawa, Japan 2003–present
surface area of site: 1594 sqm
built surface area: 170 sqm
indoor surface area: 170 sqm

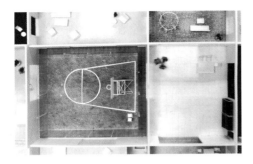

House in China, Tianjin, China 2003–present
built surface area: 610 sqm
indoor surface area: 627 sqm

Naoshima Museum, Kagawa, Japan 2005–present
with Taeko Nakatsubo, Yusuke Ohi,
Ippei Takahashi, Motoyasu Matsui
engineers: Sasaki Structural Consultants /
Mutsuro Sasaki, Tatsumi Terado,
Hirotoshi Komatsu (structural)
indoor surface area: 2,700 sqm

**Office Building, Benesse Art Site Naoshima,
Kagawa, Japan 2004**
indoor surface area: 421 sqm

Towada Museum, Aomori, Japan 2005–present
surface area of site: 4,340 sqm
built surface area: 1,920 sqm
indoor surface area: 2,300 sqm

A-House, Tokyo, Japan 2004–present
with Motoyasu Matsui, Yusuke Ohi, Ippei Takahashi
engineers: Sasaki Structural Consultants / Mutsuro Sasaki, Ayumi
Isozaki, Eisuke Mitsuda (structural); System Design Laboratory /
Takehito Sano, Akiko Sano (mechanical)
surface area of site: 123 sqm
built surface area: 72 sqm
indoor surface area: 89 sqm

biography

Kazuyo Sejima

1956

Born in Ibaraki prefecture, Japan

1981

Graduates from the Japan Women's University where she majored in Architecture

Joins Toyo Ito & Associates

1987

Establishes Kazuyo Sejima & Associates

1995

Establishes SANAA with Ryue Nishizawa

2001–present

Professor at the Keio University, Tokyo

Ryue Nishizawa

1966

Born in Kanagawa prefecture, Japan

1990

Graduates from the Yokohama National University where he majored in Architecture

Joins Kazuyo Sejima & Associates

1995

Establishes SANAA with Kazuyo Sejima

1997

Establishes the Office of Ryue Nishizawa

2001–present

Associate Professor at Yokohama National University

Exhibitions

1996

"Kazuyo Sejima + Ryue Nishizawa 1987–1996," Architectural Association School of Architecture, London, Great Britain

"Emerging Voices," Sixth International Exhibition of Architecture, Venice Biennale, Giardini di Castello, Venice, Italy

1997

"5-D Space on the Run," Swedish Museum of Architecture, Stockholm, Sweden

1998

"Kazuyo Sejima + Ryue Nishizawa," GA Gallery, Tokyo, Japan

1999

"Fancy Dance. Japanese Contemporary Art after 1990," Art Sonje Museum, Kyongiu, Korea; Art Sonje Center, Seoul, Korea

"The Un-Private House," Museum of Modern Art, New York, United States

2000

"One Hundred Thousand," Nationaltheater Station, Oslo, Norway

"Recent work of Kazuyo Sejima + Ryue Nishizawa," Harvard University, Graduate School of Design, Cambridge, Massachusetts, United States

"Less Aesthetics More Ethics," Seventh International Exhibition of Architecture, Venice Biennale, Arsenal, Venice, Italy

"Kazuyo Sejima + Ryue Nishizawa Recent Projects," Aedes Gallery, Berlin, Germany

"Kazuyo Sejima + Ryue Nishizawa Recent Projects," NAI, Rotterdam, Holland

2001

"Kazuyo Sejima + Ryue Nishizawa Recent Projects," Ministerio de Fomento, Madrid, Spain

"Roofgarden Las Palmas," Witte de With, Rotterdam, Holland

2002

"Kazuyo Sejima + Ryue Nishizawa," American Academy of Arts and Letters, New York, United States

Eighth International Exhibition of Architecture, Venice Biennale, Venice, Italy

Installation for the exhibition "Arne Jacobson – Absolutely Modern," Louisiana Museum of Modern Art, Humlebaek, Denmark

"Urban Creation Shanghai Biennale 2002," Shanghai Art Museum, Shanghai, China

2003

"Kazuyo Sejima + Ryue Nishizawa / SANAA Recent Projects," Zumtobel Staff-Lichtforum, Vienna, Austria

"Kazuyo Sejima + Ryue Nishizawa / SANAA Ampliacion del IVAM," Institut Valencia d'Art Modern, Valencia, Spain

"Kazuyo Sejima + Ryue Nishizawa / SANAA Architecture Design," Zeche Zollverein, Essen, Germany

"Kazuyo Sejima + Ryue Nishizawa / SANAA," MA Gallery, Tokyo, Japan

"Kazuyo Sejima + Ryue Nishizawa / SANAA," N Museum, Wakayama, Japan

"Kazuyo Sejima + Ryue Nishizawa / SANAA Design for a New Museum," New Museum of Contemporary Art, New York, United States

2005

"Kazuyo Sejima + Ryue Nishizawa / SANAA," Kanazawa, Japan

Awards

1998

Award of the Architectural Institute of Japan, Tokyo, Japan

2000

Erich Schelling Architekturpreis, Karlsruhe, Germany

2002

Arnold W. Brunner Memorial Architectural Award, American Academy of Arts & Letters, New York, United States

Vincenzo Scamozzi Architectural Award, Salzburg, Austria

2004

Leone d'Oro for the best work at the "Metamorph" exhibition at the Ninth International Exhibition of Architecture, Venice Biennale, Venice, Italy

2005

460th Mainichi Shimbun Arts Award (category Architecture), Japan

Rolf Schock Award (category Visual Arts), Sweden

essential bibliography

Kazuyo Sejima 1988–1996, monographic issue of *El Croquis*, 77(I), 1996

Kazuyo Sejima 1998, A.D.A. Edita, Tokyo 1998

Kazuyo Sejima 1987–1999 – Kazuyo Sejima + Ryue Nishizawa 1995–1999, monographic issue of *Japan Architect*, 35, fall 1999

SANAA / Kazuyo Sejima + Ryue Nishizawa Recent Projects, Aedes, Berlin 2000

Making the Boundary: Kazujo Sejima + Ryue Nishizawa 1995–2000, monographic issue of *El Croquis*, 99, 2000

Kazuyo Sejima in Gifu, Actar, Barcelona 2002

Kazuyo Sejima + Ryue Nishizawa / Works 1995–2003, exhibition catalogue, TOTO Shuppan, Tokyo 2003

Ocean of Air: SANAA / Kazuyo Sejima + Ryue Nishizawa 1998–2004, monographic issue of *El Croquis*, 121–22, 2004

Kazuyo Sejima + Ryue Nishizawa 2005, A.D.A. Edita, Tokyo 2005

A House in a Plum Grove, Index Communications, 2005

Kazuyo Sejima + Ryue Nishizawa / SANAA 21st Century Museum of Contemporary Art, Kanazawa, TOTO Shuppan, Tokyo 2005

Photograph Credits

We wish to thank the SANAA studios [Kazuyo Sejima + Ryue Nishizawa], Kazuyo Sejima & Associates, Office of Ryue Nishizawa, for having provided the material illustrated in this volume and for granting permission for publication.
The photographs published herein are by:

Takashi Homma: pp. 44 top, 187, 191 top, 222, 224, 225, 228

Jin Hosoya: pp. 36, 37, 44 bottom, 59, 215–17, 220, 221, 265

Nobuaki Nakagawa: pp. 172, 175, 183 bottom

Walter Niedermayr / Courtesy Gallery Koyanagi, Tokyo: pp. 10–11, 14, 15, 18, 19, 22–23, 26, 27, 30, 31

Office of Ryue Nishizawa: pp. 229 bottom, 230–35, 239, 240, 242, 243

Tomio Ohashi: pp. 104, 159, 163, 184

SANAA [Kazuyo Sejima + Ryue Nishizawa]: pp. 46, 48, 51, 54, 64, 65 bottom, 66, 67, 90, 92, 96, 97, 98, 99, 100, 103, 105, 108, 112, 118, 119, 121, 123, 130 (Brandon Hicks, Chris Hoxie, Cameron Wu), 131 (Christopher Dawson), 134 (Christopher Dawson), 135, 138–41, 146, 149

Kazuyo Sejima & Associates: pp. 158, 160, 166, 170, 178, 182, 185, 190, 191 bottom, 192, 194, 195, 198–202, 206, 208, 209 top, 210 bottom, 211

Shinkenchiku-Sha: pp. 43, 49, 50, 55, 58, 60 bottom, 61, 65 top, 162, 167, 169, 171, 179, 183 top, 203, 207, 209 bottom, 210 top, 214, 223, 229 top

Hisao Suzuki: pp. 38, 39, 42, 45, 47, 56, 57, 60 in top, 77–79, 82–85, 88, 89, 91, 93, 101, 168, 173, 174, 186, 193

Holders of rights to any unidentified photograph sources should contact the publisher.